"Dense Poems & Socratic Light"

The Poetry of John Martin Finlay
(1941–1991)

Edited by David Middleton & John P. Doucet

Wiseblood Books

Copyright © 2020 by Wiseblood Books

All rights reserved, including the right to reproduce this book or portions thereof in any form whatsoever except for brief quotations by reviewers. For information, address the publisher.

Printed in the United States of America

Set in Baskerville Typesetting
Cover Illustration by Sharon Doucet
Book Design by L. Maltese

ISBN-13: 978-0-9915832-8-7

Poetry / Literary

Wiseblood Books
Belmont, North Carolina
www.wisebloodbooks.com

John Finlay in 1968, age twenty-seven, at his writing desk in his home in Montevallo, Alabama

Acknowledgments

This new, expanded edition of the poems of John Martin Finlay includes poems that appeared in the following chapbooks and books: *The Wide Porch and Other Poems* (R.L. Barth Press, 1984); *Between the Gulfs* (Barth, 1986); *The Salt of Exposure* (The Cummington Press [Harry Duncan], 1988); *A Prayer to the Father* (Blue Heron Press, 1992); *Mind and Blood: The Collected Poems of John Finlay* (John Daniel & Company, 1992); *The American Tragedies: A Chronology of Six Poems* (Barth, 1997); and *John Finlay: A Commemoration Upon the Occasion of the Twenty-Fifth Anniversary of His Death on February 17, 1991* (Thibodaux, LA: privately printed, 2016).

Some of the poems in this edition first appeared in the following publications: *The Anglican*; *The Anglican Theological Review*; *Chasm*; *The Classical Outlook: Journal of the American Classical League*; *Comment*; *Drastic Measures*; *The Epigrammatist*; *A Garland for Harry Duncan* (W. Thomas Taylor, 1989); *Hellas: A Journal of Poetry and the Humanities* (Gerald Harnett, editor); *The Hudson Review*; *Nine Years After* (R.L. Barth, editor, R.L. Barth Press, 1989); *Louisiana English Journal*; *Order in Variety: Essays and Poems in Honor of Donald E. Stanford* (R.W. Crump, editor, 1991); *Poetry Pilot*; *Samuel Johnson: Sixteen Latin Poems Translated by Various Hands* (Barth, 1987; 1995); *Sequoia*; and *The Southern Review*. Every effort has been made by the editors to identify and contact all potential copyright holders.

The editors are also indebted to the following persons and institutions for providing materials by or about John Martin Finlay: Betty Finlay Phillips and JoAnn Finlay Hall, John Finlay's sisters and trustees of The John Finlay Literary Estate; Louisiana and Lower Mississippi Valley Collections, Hill Memorial Library, Louisiana State University, The John Finlay Papers; W.S. Hoole Special Collections Library, University of Alabama at Tuscaloosa; the Firestone Library, Princeton University; Neely Bruce; Helen Tate, for Allen Tate's letter to John Finlay; Helen Thomas, Archivist, Nicholls State University; Donald David Stanford, for the essay by his father Donald E. Stanford; David Simpson, for the essay by his father Lewis P. Simpson; Catharine Savage Brosman; Deborah Cibelli; Stella Nesanovich; David Moreland; Babs Zimmerman; and Madison Kiger, student research assistant, Nicholls State University.

Special thanks are due to Betty Finlay Phillips and JoAnn Finlay Hall for providing biographical information about their brother, John Martin Finlay, concerning some of his poems and the Finlay family, and to Angela Cybulski, Managing Editor for Wiseblood Books.

in memory

of

Patricia Sue Finlay

(November 19, 1953–March 31, 2017)

John Finlay's youngest sister,

who lovingly cared for John during his final illness

from *Origo mentis*

> It was dense poems and Socratic light,
> My endless afternoon before the war.
> Shade of the plane made water underneath
> So cool at noon, and in the summer too.
> We waded in the stream and then lay back
> Upon the sloping bank. Cicadas sang
> Those monotones of music made with fire.

For Allen Tate

> If now our lean language can sing
> Of laurel and the rough dogwood
> Caught in the single glow of faith
> That led the salty Aeneas to Rome,
> It is because of Master Tate.

On Rembrandt's Portrait of An Old Man Reading the Scriptures

> Exposure salted his grave Northern face.
> An unerasable sadness tinged that grace
> Of sourceless light glowing on solid form.
> Hard winter nights—the isolating storm—
> His oil burned out onto the living word.
> A man matured in loss, in griefs incurred
> By love outside himself, he would expend
> His mind on God, still opened to the end.

from The Autobiography of a Benedictine

> Our mind is not some Virgil cursed
> To go back down to painful shades.
> Faith dies itself and is dispersed
> In minds the deathless Word pervades.

—John Finlay

CONTENTS

Mind and Blood: The Collected Poems of John Finlay

Preface to *Mind and Blood* and
 "*Dense Poems and Socratic Light*" (2020) — 21

Preface to *Mind and Blood* (1992) — 25

The Wide Porch and Other Poems (1984)

The Wide Porch — 31
At Claybank — 32
In the Adriatic — 33
A Few Things for Themselves — 34
The Last Act — 35
Ash Wednesday — 36
The Bog Sacrifice — 37
Narcissus in Fire — 38
The Black Earth — 39
The Fourth Watch — 41
Odysseus — 42
The Archaic Athena — 43
Audubon at Oakley — 44
Three Voices After the Greek — 45

Between the Gulfs (1986)

The First Emblems — 49
Origo mentis — 50
Two Poems for Oedipus — 52
In Another Country — 53
The Case of Holmes — 54
The Defense of Solon — 55
The Inferno of the Americas — 56
The Judas Trees — 57
A Room for a Still Life — 58
Death in Asia Minor — 59
At Kerkera — 61

To a Friend on His First Book	62
Two Epigrams	63
The Dead and the Season	64
The Road to the Gulf	65

The Salt of Exposure (1988)

Under the Reign of the Actor	69
Ovid in Exile	70
For Henry James	71
Descartes in Holland	72
To a Victim of AIDS	73
A Room in Hell	74
At a Spanish Fort Near the Pensacola Naval Station	75
On the Vietnam War Memorial	76
Dunescape with a Greek Shrine	77
After Samuel Johnson's Latin Poem to Thomas Lawrence, M.D.	78
After Samuel Johnson's *Summe Pater*	79
The Blood of Shiloh	80
A Memory of the Frontier	82
The History of a Traditionalist	83
A Prayer to the Paraclete	84
On Rembrandt's Portrait of an Old Man Reading the Scriptures	85
The Autobiography of a Benedictine	86
A Pastoral of the Primitives	87
Salt from the Winter Sea	88

A Prayer to the Father (1992)

Go Little Book	93
A Prayer to the Father	94
The Faun	95
At Kalámai	96
The *Illumination* of Arthur Rimbaud	97
Baudelaire in Belgium	98
Stone and Fire	99

Flaubert in Egypt	100
A Portrait of a Modern Artist	101
The Locked Wards	102
"If a man drive out a demon . . ."	103
The End of the Affair	104
Epigrams and Briefer Lyrics	105
The Pioneers	107
Off Highway 27	108
The Seasons of the Blood	109
I Will Not Let Thee Go	110
For David During Dark Times	111

Poems from Section V of *Mind and Blood* (1992)

At Some Bar on Laguna Beach, Florida	115
The Graves by the Sea	116
The Exiles	121
In the Time of the Civil War	123
Told from the Nineteenth Century	126
Through a Glass Darkly	127
The Slaughter of the Herd	128
Aeneas in Modernity	129
Of Harry Duncan, Bookmaker	130
The Symposium for Socrates	131

Previously Uncollected Poems (2016)

133

Additional Poems, Versions of Poems, Fragments, Lines, and Related Writings from the Diaries and Other Sources

147

The American Tragedies: A Chronology of Six Poems (1987)

167

Appendices

A. Notes for the Perfect Poem by John Finlay — 181

B. The Mary Roberts Rinehart Foundation Proposal by John Finlay — 183

C. Letters Between John Finlay and Allen Tate (1966) — 186

D. A Note on John Finlay and Allen Tate by David Middleton (2018) — 190

E. A Letter from John Finlay to Janet Lewis Winters on *The American Tragedies* (1987) — 194

F. A Note on *The American Tragedies* by David Middleton (1997) — 195

G. Mind and Blood: John Finlay (1941–1991) by David Middleton (1991) — 196

H. John Finlay and the Situation of the Southern Writer by Lewis P. Simpson (1999) — 199

I. The Poetry of John Finlay by Donald E. Stanford (1991) — 214

J. "In Light Apart": The Achievement of John Finlay by David Middleton (1999) — 217

K. Preface to *John Finlay: A Commemoration Upon the Occasion of the Twenty-Fifth Anniversary of His Death on February 17, 1991* by David Middleton (2016) — 221

L. The Break-In, a poem on John Finlay by David Middleton (2016) — 224

Notes

227

John Finlay: A Bibliography (1962–2020)

267

A Note on The John Finlay Papers at Louisiana State University

273

An Entry from John Finlay's Paris Diary (1973)

275

Mind and Blood:
The Collected Poems of John Finlay
(original version; late 1980s)

To Jean Finlay

In light apart from me, I seek the Word
Holding mind and blood from the absurd.

Preface to *Mind and Blood* and "*Dense Poems and Socratic Light*" (2020)

In the twenty-eight years since *Mind and Blood* was first published in 1992, John Finlay has been recognized as an important modern poet. During that same time, more of Finlay's unpublished and uncollected work has been discovered and is now made available in a two-volume Wiseblood Books edition. This work includes essays, book reviews, a short story, poems, diaries, statements on poetics, and other literary material, as well as biographical details of Finlay's life. In 2016, some of this material was privately printed in a limited edition chapbook, chiefly for members of the Finlay family and friends of John Finlay: *John Finlay: A Commemoration Upon the Twenty-Fifth Anniversary of His Death on February 17, 1991*.

John Finlay lived just long enough to know that his literary works were highly esteemed by a number of America's and England's finest contemporary poets and scholars. *A Garland for John Finlay* (1990), presented to Finlay only three months before his death, contains poems by R. L. Barth, Edgar Bowers, Dick Davis, Dana Gioia, Helen Pinkerton, Lewis P. Simpson, Lindon Stall, Donald E. Stanford, Timothy Steele, Clive Wilmer, Janet Lewis Winters, and others.

Several years later, there appeared a special John Finlay issue of *Hellas: A Journal of Poetry and the Humanities*: "In Light Apart: The Achievement of John Finlay" (8:2, Fall/Winter 1997; book format, Glenside, PA: The Aldine Press, 1999). This volume includes "John," a poem by Edgar Bowers (winner of the Bollingen Prize for Poetry), as well as poetry and prose by Finlay himself and by other *Garland* contributors and well-known writers such as William Bedford Clark, Catharine Savage Brosman, and X. J. Kennedy.

In 1992, English poet Dick Davis succinctly made the case for Finlay's verse: "The concepts that inform Finlay's poems, the fierce, lonely Manichaeism they articulate and struggle with, are so absent from most recent poets' intellectual landscape that his seems truly a voice crying in the wilderness. And yet in their discipline and grandeur Finlay's best poems are so harrowingly beautiful that they speak to any reader with ears to hear; they deserve the minute attention of *everyone* who claims to care for the truth and craft of poetry."

A few years later, at the end of his comprehensive and judicious survey of Finlay's life and work, "The Romance of Modern Classicism: Remarks on the Life and Work of John Finlay, 1941–1991," Jeffrey Goodman offered this conclusion about Finlay's poetry at its finest: "In a number of poems Finlay came closer to writing perfect poetry, poetry that is both meaningful and moving, than anyone else of his generation has yet gotten; and the vast majority of the poems in *Mind and Blood* bear careful reading and re-reading by those who love significant and beautiful work."

To this assessment may be added remarks by Donald E. Stanford—poet, scholar, editor of *The Southern Review*, and Finlay's major professor for his Ph.D. studies at Louisiana State University. In his memorial essay in the Summer 1991 issue of *The Southern Review*, Stanford recalled a story that says much about Finlay: "Finlay was devoted to the art of poetry. Everything else appeared to be secondary in his scale of values. He would go to great lengths to meet a poet he admired. He thought the syllabic poem 'Still-Life' by the daughter of Robert Bridges, Elizabeth Daryush, was astonishingly beautiful, so off he went to meet her in her home on Boar's Hill, Oxford, England. Then he immediately returned to the States without bothering to see the sights of London."

Now, in addition to these earlier tributes by Finlay's distinguished immediate predecessors and contemporaries there has been, in the last few years, an increasing interest in Finlay the man and the artist (and especially the convert to Roman Catholicism) on the part of poets, editors, and scholars of a younger generation. Such admirers include James Matthew Wilson (currently poetry editor for *Modern Age*) and Joshua Hren (Editor-in-Chief of Wiseblood Books). And with these names should also be associated that of John P. Doucet, the coeditor both of *John Finlay: A Commemoration* (2016) and of this Wiseblood Books edition of Finlay's verse and related writings. Doucet, then in his twenties, was the youngest contributor to *A Garland for John Finlay* (1990).

This Wiseblood Books edition of Finlay's poetry, along with its companion volume of Finlay's prose, should provide both the scholar and the general reader with materials for a more comprehensive view of Finlay's life and works than has heretofore been possible. Finlay once said that he wanted to write poetry that was "just above the level of prose." And, conversely, it may be said that Finlay's prose often displays in concentration the subtler rhythms and more vivid images most often associated with poetry. Ideally, the poetry and prose should be read together as the fullest record now in print of Finlay's life and literary art.

This new edition of John Finlay's poems and related writings begins with the original *Mind and Blood* whose contents, title, and epigraph were chosen by Finlay himself. Late revisions Finlay made in 1988 to some of his earlier poems in *Mind and Blood* have been incorporated here. Finlay clearly intended this book, in this version— left completed but unpublished at his death—to be his collected poems, the volume on which he would stake his reputation.

In the 1992 edition of *Mind and Blood*, the editor added, as indicated in a Note to the Preface, a Section IV and a Section V to Finlay's original typescript (Sections I-III). The poems in Section IV, found among Finlay's papers after his death, were composed between the mid-1960s and the spring of 1990. Except for "At Some Bar on Laguna Beach, Florida, Winter, 1969," the uncollected poems in Section V were all published during the 1980s. This Wiseblood Books edition restores *Mind and Blood* to its final state as determined by Finlay himself very near the end of his life.

The uncollected and unpublished poems from Sections IV and V of the 1992 edition of *Mind and Blood* appear here now separately but in their original ordering by the editor of the 1992 edition. These poems Finlay wrote as a fully mature poet. To this verse have been added earlier poems—published but uncollected—as well as unpublished verse, verse-fragments, earlier versions, lines, and related writings either found in Finlay's papers or obtained from other sources. Some of these poems, especially those from the early to the mid 1960s, are not the work of a fully mature poet. Nevertheless, they are an important record of Finlay's poetic development and should now be made available to scholars of Finlay's work. Dates of composition or publication of these earlier poems are given when known.

Also presented separately here is *The American Tragedies*, originally a chapbook of poems chosen and sequenced by Finlay in 1987. An appendix below contains the editor's note to the 1997 printing of this chapbook as well as Finlay's letter to poet Janet Lewis Winters (1899–1998) to whom Finlay sent a typescript of this collection and to some of whose verse Finlay's six poems seem to be indebted. Poems in this chapbook sometimes differ significantly from their revised versions in *Mind and Blood*.

There are several other appendices to this volume. These appendices contain documents both by and about Finlay, especially concerning his poetry, poetics, and poetic development. Of special note are the two previously unpublished letters between Finlay and the distinguished southern man of letters, Allen Tate (1899–1979). Prefaces and notes by the editor were composed over many years for different occasions and purposes. There is, inevitably, some repetition of material, including quotations from Finlay's poems, but it seemed best, for the record, to leave these pieces just as they were originally written.

The Notes section provides the reader with some biographical, historical, and literary information that may be of help when read in conjunction with the poems. Much about John Finlay's life remains to be discovered and recorded. A full-scale biography and a critical, even a variorum, edition of the poems will be a worthy project for scholars of a future generation.

Finally, there is a selected bibliography of works both by and about Finlay, a note on The John Finlay Papers at Louisiana State University, and, in closing, an entry from the diary Finlay kept in Paris in 1973. This diary entry seemed to the editors to be an appropriate way to conclude this Wiseblood Books edition of Finlay's verse and related writings.

—David Middleton, editor of *Mind and Blood* (1992) and literary executor for John Finlay

Preface to *Mind and Blood* (1992)

John Martin Finlay was born in his maternal grandmother's house in Ozark, Alabama, on January 24, 1941. His parents, Tom Coston Finlay and Jean Sorrell Finlay, owned a peanut and dairy farm outside the nearby town of Enterprise, and there John Finlay spent his early youth coming to know firsthand the mystery, the beauty, and the hardship of agricultural life. He also became a deep and avid reader, sometimes reciting passages of Shakespeare to the cows (whom he named after Greek goddesses) as he took them to and from the pasture every day.

After finishing public school in Enterprise, Finlay earned his B.A. (1964) and M.A. (1966) in English at the University of Alabama at Tuscaloosa and taught for four years at the University of Montevallo. Then, in 1970, Finlay entered the doctoral program at Louisiana State University in order to study under Donald E. Stanford, editor of *The Southern Review* and former student of Yvor Winters. Along with Allen Tate, Winters was one of Finlay's primary models of the poet-critic that he himself aspired to be.

Except for the years 1972–73, which he spent on the Greek island of Corfu and in Paris, Finlay was at LSU throughout the 1970s. He received the Ph.D. in December of 1980 after completing his dissertation on Yvor Winters' intellectual theism. He also joined the Roman Catholic Church in 1980.

In 1981, Finlay left Baton Rouge for the family farm in Alabama where for ten years he wrote essays, reviews, and new poems. On February 17, 1991, John Finlay died of AIDS, leaving behind his unpublished book of essays on the Gnostic spirit in modern literature—*Flaubert in Egypt and Other Essays*—as well as three published chapbooks of poems, the typescript of his collected poems—*Mind and Blood*—, unpublished and uncollected poems, three essays from an unfinished book on the Greeks, and several diaries kept in Enterprise, in Tuscaloosa, on Corfu, in Paris, and in Baton Rouge.

Finlay's poems are almost all in traditional literary forms. He mainly wrote plain-style lyrics of direct statement, short narratives, and post-symbolist poems whose sensuous details exhibit controlled associationism in which definite ideas and feelings are indirectly yet logically presented. Whether plain-style, narrative, or post-symbolist, Finlay's poems are serious, simple, deep, direct, and often traumatically revealing of the human condition. The best of them are truly unforgettable.

Finlay addresses such subjects as the origin of the mind, the relation of mind and matter, mind and the irrational, the mind and God, the nature of evil, Thomistic theology, philosophical subjectivism, the inscrutability and beauty of the natural world, primitive religious rituals, and, especially in the later poems, family life in the South since the early nineteenth century, Indian life in the South, the nature of modern war, and the isolation of the serious thinker and artist in the contemporary world.

Particularly impressive are poems in which these themes are confronted by one or another of Finlay's heroes of the mind including Odysseus, Oedipus, Solon, the exiled Ovid, a Benedictine monk, Samuel Johnson, Audubon, Henry James, or Sherlock Holmes and poems in which characters such as Narcissus, Spanish gold-hunters, Descartes, and Rimbaud suffer various forms of self-delusion which warp or destroy their moral nature. Among Finlay's most poignant and tragic figures are those who, through madness or disease, allow us to see beyond their suffering and unawareness the divinely ordained, objective moral grounding of the world. Examples of such characters are the mad women in "The Locked Wards," the shattered Confederate veteran in "The Blood of Shiloh," and the hate-filled, natural-law-denying novelist in "A Portrait of a Modern Artist."

Among John Finlay's papers (now at LSU) is a remarkable prose statement written to accompany an (unsuccessful) application to a foundation for financial assistance to provide the poet time to research and write a long narrative poem on Audubon. In this statement, which amounts to a poetic credo, Finlay says: "1 do not intend for [the poem] to be a loose, vaguely subjective account of this cunning, single-minded Frenchman. I hope that it will be rooted in history and fact, and evolve from actual observation of Audubon's wilderness, or the little that is left of it today. This does not mean that it will be unpoetic. For me the greatest poetry comes, not from fantasy, but from intense, realistic perceptions of the natural and human worlds." Finlay goes on to discuss the central idea of the proposed poem: "The theme is the immersion of Audubon's mind and art in the American wilderness of the 19th century, his recovery from it, and then the discipline and passion necessary to understand the experience and translate its beauty into art. Audubon is the prototype of the artist, who has to shift back and forth between two sometimes conflicting worlds: the experience of the wilderness, immediate, sensual, non-intellectual, and the mental state of detachment from that experience, in which the mind works through the wilderness into art."

Finlay never wrote his longer poem, but he did write a fine shorter poem on Audubon. A late paragraph in Finlay's statement is related to this poem: "the last part will be much the longest and broadest in scope. Here [Audubon] realizes his art and makes his first really significant breakthrough. . . . We see him in his semi-intuitive, semi-intellectual contact with the raw, even primitive aspects of the wilderness, and observe the cunning and craft he used to get his prey and then to reproduce the almost inexplicable mystery of its livingness, the actual look in the mockingbird's eye as it hovers in the air, poised, its wings outspread, ready to fight the rattlesnake coiled tightly around its nest." This mysterious struggle of the artist to do justice to the objective world is captured in the final lines of the completed "Audubon at Oakley":

> I saw my book, taut wings of mockingbirds
> In combat with the snake knotted beneath
> The nest, its open mouth close to the eggs,
> Now held forever in the lean, hard line.
> And underneath, defining them, combined:
> The clean abstraction of their Latin names,
> The vulgate richness of this Saxon salt.

Now held forever in the lean, hard line. Readers who want serious poems that vividly present sensuous experience as understood by a mature mind steeped in classical and Christian tradition, yet fully aware of the problems of the contemporary world and of the perpetual threat of the primitive and the irrational, should find much to their liking in *Mind and Blood*. In their severe and uncompromising grandeur John Finlay's best poems are surely permanent additions to American literature.

—David Middleton

The Wide Porch and Other Poems (1984)

John Finlay as a child on "the wide porch" of his maternal grandmother's house in Ozark, Alabama

THE WIDE PORCH

For M. C. F. [1]

Where nothing can be other than it was,
I hold the house as solid in my mind
As it had been before it was destroyed.
Standing in sycamore, live-oak and pine,
Still the seasons soak its holding frame.

Sasanquas blooming in the winter sun,
Air cool inside like water from a well
As summers peeled the painted walls outside,
Fall rains sounding in the rooms all night—
These laved and filled the backward mind.

I see our family on the wide porch,
In sun that thickens to a wilderness—
The upper columns seethed in summer bees—
And know the past encoded in the blood
As deaths perfected it and sealed it up.

I swept away the clotted leaves and dirt
From graves my uncle took me out to clean.
The massive autumns drunk in their own seed,
Staining the chilled slabs, nothing underneath—
I then moved outward to become myself.

She who last lived there, finally alone,
Died terrified, flesh holding on to flesh.
No cries came when that agony had ceased.
We closed her eyes, transfixed in nothingness,
Then left her covered in the naked light.

I left the house. The sun was rising keen
In burning fog away from each bright leaf.
A swimmer coming out of blinding salt,
I stared where trees stood rooted in a world
Brutal and calming in the clearing sun.

AT CLAYBANK [2]

Your parents lie buried
Under emblems of waves.
Cold surges of granite
Secure the ancient graves.

After pain and blindness,
With clouds closing in,
Summer lightning and rain,
We bring you to your kin.

What you asked is done.
You lie in their pure flood.
The rain washes the clay
Above it, dark as blood.

IN THE ADRIATIC [3]

In translucent night, rising from the sea,
The coastal mountains ended in the moon.
Up to their heights, cultivated groves
Held them in place. Under reflecting leaves,
The turning undersides of thin pale fish,
The twisted olive trunks were rooted deep.
Miles down, in isolated clefts of rock,
As in a well, black water sucked the base.

A FEW THINGS FOR THEMSELVES [4]

Along the bay live-oaks and magnolias
Gather massively the warm blackness
As birds dart and cry in their hard leaves.

At their base the narrow strip of beach
Is yellow and African in the late sun.
We hold off and let the boat drift. . . .

The string of fish in the bottom
Lies in spilled oil, blood and bay-water.
Their white underbellies gleam in the dusk.

A black watersnake is moving into
The closed, muscle-like blooms of lilies,
The darker swamp weeds along the shore.

Slowly we follow it, back to the dock.
And walk in the early night through crickets,
The low wind in the rusty screens.

THE LAST ACT

> *'Tis the god Hercules, whom Antony loved,*
> *Now leaves him.* [5]

It is too often only close to death,
Or utter failure, when the mind is held
To truth, we see the outlines of the gods,
Those whom we loved but never realized.
Above us in a void burnt-out and cold,
At unfamiliar heights their forms return
Like ghosts to move across the final night,
Remote and unappeased in our collapse.
There is no bitterness in facing them.
The heart that fatally kept them deprived,
And saw them hostile to the living blood,
Will pay in blood its error, every vein.
In what is not the gods are reconfirmed,
The candor of their presence briefly seen.
The tragedy leaves nothing else but that.
Then they are gone. The music underground,
The quiet terror of its shifting source,
Its echoes vanishing, moves in their place.

ASH WEDNESDAY [6]

The floor is cold on which I kneel. Unclaimed
As yet by any grace, I try my mind
On rottenness and sin revealed and named
By law, but hear within the loosening bind
Of flesh, instead, determined in its plight
The spoiling heart irrelevant and tight.

THE BOG SACRIFICE [7]

The iron and acid water of the bog,
Rising and falling with the winter rains,
Two thousand years, preserved him as he died,
Pinned naked to the floor by wooden crooks.
No fire had cut and cleaned the clotted soul.
Runic stakes, washed white as salt, were laid
Over his narrow breast, sunk in the peat.

The sacrificial rope they hanged him from,
Of woven skins, still cut into his throat,
Tight as when death came. His gentle face,
Forced upward by the torsion of the noose,
Bore with monstrous discipline his bane,
As loose ends, like serpents, meandered down
His naked length, pressed into his flesh.

A cap of wolfskin hived his shaven head.
Descended from a line of conscript priests,
He died in youth, still delicate and whole.
When he was lifted from the pit, the earth
Itself then sweating like an ancient beast,
He looked as if alive. Faint cries of snipes
Brought sunlight piercing to his closing eyes.

Before Christ reached this isolated north,
A chthonic goddess, holding iron breasts,
Each year in early spring exacted death.
In winter when the winds blew keen off ice,
Or summer with its rippling swarm of weeds,
The bog seemed never raised above the sea,
But underneath, out of whose depths she came.

NARCISSUS IN FIRE [8]

He moved apart. For nights in solitude
He watched his mind, in anguish at itself,
Exhaust the will and, burning in its own
Locked speed, turn into itself, deprived
Of those objective forms sustaining life.
He saw the blackness breed another scheme,
Himself the landscape surfacing brute waste.
And stared into its moon until his eye,
An open pulse, beat in the rustic fire.

THE BLACK EARTH

In the beginning was a crime...
—Hannah Arendt, *On Revolution* [9]

Toward dawn a dusty mirror frames the moon.
With lines cut on the surface of the glass,
I watch it rising like a fire in space.
The walls of my small room are burnt away.
Like prehistoric time the past floods up—
Fields rising in moonlight from solid oak,
Swamps where lidlessly the snake slid down
Gutted banks, pine-quiet, into the light.

The moon was god. Its white compulsive fire,
Reflected from the pits of scattered seas,
Transfixed the eye and cut the veinless core.
To keep from savage sleep, at nights I clung
To what one light left burning in the house
Saved of my room. I stayed above the dream,
Until the mental walls and floors dissolved
Against my will, and mind and light were lost.

I killed the father in the mangled dream,[10]
A wasted man who strained his cruel life
Taut as barb-wire pulled on rigid posts.
His fields stood bearded under summer noons.
I dreamed instead the fall, the rotten wheat
Uncut, the sound of hawks in foreign skies,
The father found alive on the black earth,
The blindness made by me to hide the crime.

As punishment, the breaking mind absorbed
Into its very blood his bloodless ghost.
I woke in sweat. The open window framed
The steady light, the bare, distended skin
Of earth on fire outside the narrow room.
I fought to hear the scream I kept inside,
But still, a naked thing, I heard his voice
At once both curse and cry, condemning me.

The moon has risen white. The mirror clears
Of darker fire. His voice now fades like pain

A human takes, absorbs, and then survives.
This moon itself will fade, whose cobalt glow
The dawn soon strikes to almost nothingness.
Throughout morning it will but faintly gleam
There in the west, a disc of thin white bone,
The center eaten through with constant light.

THE FOURTH WATCH [11]

> ... *and about the fourth watch of the night he cometh unto them, walking upon the sea.* ...
> —Mark 6:48

No fictive dawn discloses me some god,
The foam of rabid wolves, the guts of fish
Kept from his tomb not fixed in any sod,
Where nothing speaks whatever is his wish.
In light apart from me, I seek the Word
Holding mind and blood from the absurd.

At every move some bruised, malignant part
Of me, that evil I have not withstood,
But found instead within the viscid heart,
Resists the sequent meaning of the good.
A lightning screen of images stays time
To fix me in a wordless past still blind.

You made us out of nothing, primal Word.
Not lost or spilt in uncreated waste,
My essence is not You by matter blurred.
But nothing leaves in me its mortal taste.
I am because of You. And in Your claim
I find my life and speak Your holy name.

On earth You spoke to heal demonic men
Begging wholeness in the splitting tomb,
Who saw You out as God through utter sin.
The sea beyond the will, archaic spume,
Night's fourth watch below the human mind,
You also calmed and left to its own kind.

Embedded mind sustains the complex whole
Redeemed with blood of Deity made flesh—
You save the man, not disembodied soul.
And summer burns the tireless sun afresh:
A wedding-feast out under shade of limes,
The servants brimming water-jars with wine!

ODYSSEUS

In honor of Yvor Winters [12]

I could not know the meaning of that time
I lay long nights upon those rotting planks
To hear the wind blow wild in shredded sails,
Until I heard the voyage beat out in words.
When the blind poet ceased, I went outside [13]
And stared down slopes below encrusted walls
Whose stone absorbed the cries of closing surf.
From where I stood I saw, at its low edge,
The narrow beach that, momently submerged,
Withstood the wide explosions of the tide.

THE ARCHAIC ATHENA [14]

Small owls in the spring nights
Whirr through pines below her shrine.

The new-skinned snake sleeps
Full-fed in its temple cage.

Her wooden statue washed in the sea
Gazes through foam of the moon.

Wisdom knows the grasping root
Ending as thinnest hair in waters

Held pure and trembling in a well.

AUDUBON AT OAKLEY

My Gallic cunning poured sweet wine into
The calyxes of trumpet-vines and caught
Small drunken birds a bullet blows apart.
Others I shot, pinned them to a board
To draw the fresh-killed life. Elusively,
The *is* that quickens in the living eye
Escaped the sweat of art, drying ink.
I tore blind pages till I reached the one
That pleased my avid mind. The wilderness
There teems with birds I never saw before:
White and wood ibises, the sparrow hawk,
The red-cock woodpecker, and painted finch.
I hunted them for days and nights until
I throve in timelessness. One day stood out.
I heard below all things the river sough;
The fall was blazing in the silent trees.
I saw my book, taut wings of mockingbirds
In combat with the snake knotted beneath
The nest, its open mouth close to the eggs,
Now held forever in the lean, hard line.
And underneath, defining them, combined:
The clean abstraction of their Latin names,
The vulgate richness of this Saxon salt.

THREE VOICES AFTER THE GREEKS [16]

Archilochus [17]

1. *Between battles*

Bring wine that has a bitter bite
And thickest oak to burn through night.
Forget the dead, the vultured tree,
The other deaths that soon must be.
My soul, stay firm through all of this.
My only strength is drunkenness.

2.

You dainty officer, poor muscle fool,
Keep flashing that unbloodied sword of yours
At these crude asses in this savage Thrace:
You'll finally get it stiff as any boor's.

Sappho [18]

1.

What is most lovely? Some say cavalries
Of Asia, teaming chariots, or fleets,
Winds spreading sails in turgid strength.
But I say what one loves. How plain to see!

2.

Cool water ripples through the blooming
trees, this spring air, and falls
in ceaseless waves on my pliant flesh,
Goddess out of the spume on depths!

Callimachus [19]

Don't come to me for bolts and thunder.
Zeus is the clerk for all that lumber.

Between the Gulfs (1986)

THE FIRST EMBLEMS [20]

Veins of sea-
weed, thin
bones of fossil
fish, the print
of shells in stone
turned inward
to the core.
Gulleys choked
with kudzu.
Miles down
the bleached road,
the hot salt
and the white
Gulf at noon.

ORIGO MENTIS [21]

I was the bastard, or the younger son,[22]
The immigrant, suspicious and detached,
Who left the womb of crowded villages
For seas no rooted mother-god could cross,
And off barbaric coasts of Asia sought
My white star rising in the moonless heat,
Island cities of my breathless birth! [23]

*

And yet no place explains my origin.
The tender, gut-like smoothness of inside
The brain a barrier of bone defends.
There I fuse with matter, human flesh,
And apprehend the essence and the thing.
If I am ruthless with most mysteries,
The knotted one I cannot solve is self.

*

One lightning bolt of abstract thought
Defined godhead so clearly that it left
The primal gods exhausted by the earth,
Enormous buttocks, faceless heads of sex,
The dying god, his seed at any cost.
It ended too the worship of the dead.
When what is deathless makes the argument,
Nothing mortal can survive its point.
I burned the body others kept and begged.

*

But nothing is forgot, an irony
That bitters me at times. Once conceived,
Its image lives in Hades of the mind,
The elegiac night of formless tombs
And speechless absence hot as brutal fact.
One drop of me though changes everything.

*

It was dense poems and Socratic light,
My endless afternoon before the war.
Shade of the plane made water underneath
So cool at noon, and in the summer too.
We waded in the stream and then lay back
Upon the sloping bank. Cicadas sang
Those monotones of music made with fire.[24]

TWO POEMS FOR OEDIPUS [25]

I.

You blind King Oedipus, emblem of mind,
In whom Apollo sunk those awful claws,[26]
No fate forced you to learn your crimes.
The god left free kinetic intellect,
Deathless, matterless, itself like god,
Which cuts like acid to a final cause.
You chose and seized yourself the agony
Of kingship, goat-song of purest law. [27]
Unshadowed noon, the isolated throne,
Clearing of marble lit by reason's god—
You held these blinded in your sacrifice.

II.

For all the oracle compelled you to,
You could have been some faun in Thebes,
Full of warm experience, and simply died.
You once saw in a barn at night an old
Bull's innocent eyes lifted to a lamp,
The buried roof above him sifting snow,
And felt a moment's kinship to the brute
As totally you drank his essence up,
Poseidon's bull, the sea as solid flesh! [28]

IN ANOTHER COUNTRY [29]

Untouched in his reserve and luminous,
The self I could have been yet never was,
Stared half-conscious of my being there.
Discovered in the autumn woods, he sat
In the dry grass, finished with the kill,
Resting for the final walk toward home.
A mess of dove and quail lay at his feet,
The rifle gleaming in the level sun.

As if he waited awkward for my other fate,
The mind abandoned then on open earth,
And knew the justice of its stranger life,
He moved, evading me, into the closing dark.
And, in his place, the other self awoke
In the fierce sunlight of a foreign room.

THE CASE OF HOLMES [30]

The *scientific searcher* scans the blood,[31]
The objects in the room, the tracks of mud,
Thickest around the pathos of the corpse.
He doesn't let instinctual grief that warps
The vision cause him not to find that fact
Which later hangs the murderer. Abstract
And lean, he seems emotionless cold thought,
Almost at times as sexless, always taut.
He has to drug a mind that will not cease
Once a case is solved—cocaine's release,
Or trance before the chemical blue flame.
And there are states of mind he cannot name,
As skulking in the fog, urban night-wood,
He feels compressed, erotic brotherhood
And for the hardest criminal. But these
Are freakish states and disappear. He sees
Himself as whole in this: revulsion for
The *great malignant brain* who wages war [32]
On those who break an ego's brutal dream.
He matches brain to brain in the extreme
Of hot collected nerves and cold reserve.
Fear also makes him whole; he must preserve
One being in the conflict with that brain
Or else, at one mistake, he will be slain.

THE DEFENSE OF SOLON [33]

Black earth, the mother of immortal gods,
Be my bond that what I speak is truth.
I pulled out of your sacred soil the stakes
Of land-enslaving predators and healed
Your wound back in the ancient families.
To Athens, citadel of light, I called
Back home those exiles sold in slavery,
Whose being was debased in foreign tongues.
I freed the Greeks oppressed by Greeks
And broke the rabid force of brutal men.
I never was afraid of power. I fused
It with strict justice, disregarding blood,
And made a rod I used to rule the state.
Justice bade me pay homage to the whole.
The sun-struck body gleaming in its sweat,
Its health confirmed in agony of games,
But body lit with light of ruling mind—
That image formed my model for the laws.
And yet I had no peace. The broken parts
Of faction begged me ceaselessly to force
Myself as ruthless tyrant on the state
So they could live off me like parasites.
I knew that solitude in tyrants' souls,
Their only friends the thugs of bodyguards,
Their only life a dream of purest fear
Disguised as arrogance and endless greed.
I fought them off and held tenaciously
The juster mean excluding mad extremes
And in the end I was reviled by everyone.
But yet I cannot think that I have failed
Though Athens chose the tyrants after me.
I wrote the laws on everlasting stone.[34]
I did not leave them on the heart or trust
Their substance to the memories of men.
They will survive my private death in time
And Athens' slavery now proves their truth.

THE INFERNO OF THE AMERICAS [35]

We floated by islands never seen
By human eyes. Perfume of their trees
Stunned the sense in the wild sun.

Sudden transparencies disclosed
The ocean's depths—we hung beguiled,
Like gods drunk on this universe.

At night we saw the stars, myths
Of the old houses, burn up and flake [36]
In phosphor on the lunar sea.

The green and white tree-boas.
With two lungs and vestiges of claws,
Choked the upper trunks of ceibas [37]

Under which on land we moved
And found the gold of naked Adam,
White bones in eternal heat.

THE JUDAS TREES [38]

I saw she had come back from hell itself—
Sweat clung to her delicate white face
Whose fine bones haunted me as a small boy.
Her voice again I heard in the dry air,
Gentle yet precise as her ironic brain:
"How can you live through your absurdity,
Religious pain? Hell at least is pure."
Scorn still ate the vitals of her soul;
A sexless tenderness burned in her eyes.
"I heard for weeks my brother beg to die.
I felt his pain. I hated God that night
I killed a living corpse to give him peace."
She lived alone and kept ferocious dogs;
She read her Virgil and the Civil War—
The seed of Troy in the young Confederates
Killed by Yankee Greeks, the women sold
As barren slaves to a vulgar modern fate.[39]
But in her lonely mind that murdered God
She was just as modern as all the rest.
The last time I saw her alive she looked
Defined in death. Protected by her dogs,
She showed me an old garden she still kept,
The Judas trees blooming beside the wall,
Buds of quince among the gleaming thorns.
She nearly stumbled, blinded in the sun,
The vernal light reflected from the soil,
But held her balance as I reached for her.
"Do not touch me if I do fall," she said.
"These dogs of mine will eat you up alive."

A ROOM FOR A STILL LIFE [40]

Delicate stalks meander through blue silk
Rootlessly and float blooms white as milk
Upon the sofa's green. The polished floor
Reflects the island of the room the more
Pelagic light pours through a wall of glass.[41]
Some books of images are stacked *en masse*
Beside an open clock. Light thickens now;
The colors change; a copper gold somehow
Like acid etches things, an unseen knife,
The cliffs of vividness, mortal still life.
The modish woman lifts her head to face
The god across the room. A circle base
Supports his damaged body; rods connect
His shattered thighs; each part is flecked
With minute stain. But yet the pieces hold,
Become themselves pure art, imagined mold,
In her acute though cool aesthetic mind.
It is the fragment, something not defined
But felt through nerves outside the whole,
Which satisfies and gives her mind its sole
And isolated act these days. Time seems
The kind of autumn light one sees in dreams,
Which floods a fictive object she had made,
Which floods her too against a wider shade.

DEATH IN ASIA MINOR [42]

At a Coastal Shrine in the 2nd Century, A.D.

Indigo feathers of the slaughtered cocks,
Against white marble, blacken in the chill
Late afternoon. A priest will burn them soon
Within the precincts of this god who dies.
The bowls, the whetted sacrificial knives,
Already washed of blood, gleam in the studs
With sunlight failing in the circled shrine.
The bearded image, with the dog and snake,
Stares lidless at the columned yard outside
Where frost is thickening on the bare ground.
Water brims, nervously is poised in pools
Fed by the springs erupting underneath.
Below the cliff, the winter sea cries out,
The shrine invaded by the constant sound
Which mounts into the quiet brain to make
In them at night, entranced within the god,
Low undertows of noise.
                      The men extreme
Who stay all night, have purified themselves,
In thinnest water cleansed demonic flesh.
They lie, some with knives, on narrow beds,
Locked inside a room sealed off from light,
Sifting dissolving fragments of the brain
To find this distant god who comes in blind
Destruction of the mind. Each strains to be
The shipless winter sea, or timeless fire
That eats itself alive, the human knot
Dissolved or burnt, in water or in fire.

The oldest dreams again he hears the wind,
Crying in frozen trees, before the dawn,
When he had stared abstracted at the tide—
The whole wave pulled to pieces by the moon—
Then bled himself, according to the dream
Wherein the god had spoken through the wind.
As he awakes, though blind as when he slept,
The thawing sun, which smokes itself into
A frozen world, lies cindered in his mind.
He stands on ice and sees the nervous threads
Of blood, again, unskeining from the gash.
The dawn repeats the sea, now leveled flat,
Solid in livid blue, like trembling slag,
The broken banks, the cries of preying gulls.
The rind of self now burning in the god,
Nothing reclaims his gutted mind, a skull
Soon cleaned, the body drained, cast in a grave
To break and darken, costing him no pain.

AT KERKERA [43]

Erosive waves cut knives
Spining this spur of rock.
Above, walled strata lock
A shrine in solid hives.

No one can go inside
Its jutting room to see
The Christ in agony
Or know His end alive.

We live below His death.
He waits for us enshrined.
The dark iconic mind
Feeds on mortal breath.

TO A FRIEND ON HIS FIRST BOOK [44]

How strange seeing your poems in a book.
I once could feel the pathos of those nights
About them still in hottest Baton Rouge,
Black coffee, poverty, the sweated line!
They only are themselves in this rich book.
I read them as a stranger, not a friend—
Poems get deathless, out of our control—
And see the man who started them consumed.

TWO EPIGRAMS

I. *The Hunter*

What I kill my folk live on for life.
What I slay I must respect to prove
My skill and stoic calm in deadly strife.
I get the wound in what cold seasons move.

II. *A Fragment for the Fall*

In the slanting gap of night black crickets
Keep at their song on the lean earth and frost.
All night a full moon burns the bare thickets,
The skin of earth, the river blind and lost.

THE DEAD AND THE SEASON

To my uncle killed in a farming accident during the Fifties

The western sides of barns stay oven-hot
Where insects glue the tight cocoon of eggs—
Air blowing off the Gulf, the pouring sun!
Fire has cleaned off stubble from the fields;
What once was yours lies fallow in the light.
Late autumn afternoons your mother dreams
That you come back. *How can it ever change?*,
She asks out in the dusk of settled gold,
The dead, the season fused inside her soul.

But change will come. Under the iron sky
The winter oats will grow on frozen earth.
This dawn we pulled a heifer's early calf—
One leg bent backwards clogged the passageway.
We cleared its nostrils of the viscous film
So it could breathe. The mother's afterbirth
And broken blood lay steaming in the chill.

Why am I telling you this?, you dead
These many years and surely now indifferent,
Or arrogant, to things involving blood.
In one full night you paid the mortal debt
On sheets soaked through, then never changed.
Why would you now come back? We ourselves
Deserted you. We shunned for rawest guilt
What seemed pure evil in your bloodless face
So that your end was strangers and a priest.
We lived the remnant of that morning blurred:
The chilled and silent house, engulfing light,
Some neighbors who had come to cook our meal,
The slugs of scalding whiskey for our blood.

THE ROAD TO THE GULF

A small white town, its silver water-tank
Gleaming above a green deep river's bank,
We passed before the pastures still unmowed
And melons piled for sale beside the road.
Samples were cut on shells of oyster blue,
So ripe the seedless heart had split in two.
The closer to the Gulf we came the more
The flattened earth recalled itself as shore.
The needle of the pine, metallic leaf,
Grew where lusher life would come to grief.
The soil lay dreaming of the ancient salt,
A trance of heat inside the summer's vault.
It cooled by evening when we reached the bay.
Blacked vistas opened out; just miles away,
We felt the plunging shelves of rising sea.
The boats were in; at shore beneath a tree
The scaling boys half-naked, brown as nuts,
Threw to the blue crabs the fishes' guts.

The Salt of Exposure (1988)

UNDER THE REIGN OF THE ACTOR [46]

Cocaine and money cure and fix our wills.
He makes us little gods for other ills.

OVID IN EXILE [47]

The frigid Bear-star ranges near the place [48]
Where now I try to live among a savage race.
My exile lies north of the crucial straits
That flow between my Europe and those gates
Of Asia, north where the edges of the world
Fall off in bearding ice and hang uncurled.
The unmapped inlets of the fierce Black Sea
Wash through my open prison. I live free
Where Roman grace has never drawn the soul
Or taught its basest motions self-control.
Winter lets down the upper hordes who cross
The frozen Ister that, liquid, was a fosse.[49]
Witches made poisons for their arrow-tips.
Death-hunger goads them on and Mars equips [50]
Their shrunken minds with fury for the kill.
After they leave, these villages stay still
For hours; survivors then emerge from holes
And cremate murdered kin on oak and coals.
It is the white, void endlessness of snow
That seals the mind inside, and fungi grow
Within its darkened core. My Roman life,
My poems' fame and friends, my absent wife,
All seem absurd, unreal. I strain in tears
To focus on their forms. Among my fears,
The chief is of their death in my own mind.
To keep my Latin pure and still enshrined,
Like someone crazed, I talk out loud alone.
I but half learn the gutteral harsh groan,
The snarl of spit they use as human speech.
They think the poet queer, a woman-screech
Who froths beneath the madness of the moon,
Who best is simply killed off in her swoon.
I hide my poems from these vulgar tribes.
And still I write—my muse alone inscribes
Some peace, some reason on my lonely rage.
I then am steeled to finish through my age.
If Caesar should forbid me still my home,
My death lies here. My poems live in Rome.[51]

FOR HENRY JAMES [52]

You stared at, as you died,
the warships on the Thames,
gigantic blank hulks
of steel bound to a war
blinded to your distinctions—
your last discovery of Europe.

How far away they seemed,
the great summer houses. . . .
Against the richest light
on old lichened walls,
all through those afternoons,
limpid, suffused with gold,
the endless talk went on.

And afterwards, in the pools
of candlelight, among
cut-flowers in huge vases,
the tall French windows
closed against the night,
not one gesture betrayed
your own beast of deprivation,
waiting in the scented air,
eluding even you.

How private you became. . .
with nothing left at the end—
no Europe or America—
but stoic courtesy,
death a *distinguished thing*.[53]

DESCARTES IN HOLLAND [54]

He did not care to understand one word
The burghers said, and let thick fog create
A whiteness rendering his eyes absurd—
He had his mind inside for purer fate.

TO A VICTIM OF AIDS

Nurses who come near you wear masks,
As if your flesh breathed fatal germs.
They act absorbed by routine tasks,
As if there were, for them, no terms
For what it's now your eyes that ask.

The dark back rooms you sucked cock in,
The prolonged sweat of "river-rats,"
Of what you called "tight city-skin"—
The dudes, the studs, the alley-cats—
Destroyed the man that you had been.

You scorned judgement—pure tyranny,
You said, of some cold, proud elite—
Yet were the slave as you set free
The lord of flies, who swarms the meat
Of self-despair, your sex in debris.

Your body became your state of soul.
It can't condemn one thing, but must
Permit what comes, with no control.
The germ not killed now breeds in lust
On its own self, and kills the whole.

A ROOM IN HELL

In this tinted half-light
The snake scar of error
Is blurred; careful insight
Intoxicates itself.

The surf of phantasies,
Drenching deathless mind,
Dissolves rigidities,
The little we had been.

Outside, the soul's sleet
Whispers the warp of ice.
Further out, waves beat
Themselves apart and cry.

AT A SPANISH FORT
NEAR THE PENSACOLA NAVAL STATION [55]

Black cannons of this coastal fort
Lie silent now. The mouth of fire
Is filled with vines; bees make report
In powdered blooms which they desire.

The fort had stood three centuries
Guarding the entrance to the bay.
Vain in our pure war's totalities,
It falls to myth and thick decay.

Our warriors are freed from earth,
Angelic, clean, new minds which hate
Those limits of our mundane birth,
Which soar outside the mesh of fate.

We hardly see the whitening jet
Straining toward the blinding sun.
Our mind can only sense its threat
In sound, its screaming loaded run.

ON THE VIETNAM WAR MEMORIAL [56]

The dead's full names are cut
On depthlessness of glass—
The long war's human glut
On naked walls in grass.

They cut slab in bare fact,
Like graves without a cross.
Their art could not abstract
One meaning from the loss.

DUNESCAPE WITH A GREEK SHRINE

The further dunes receive the pounding sea.
        They never stay the same—
        Both wind and wave constrain
Their shapeless drifts so they can never be.

They are the graves of trash washed up by the sea,
        The whitened battlefield
        Where moon and ocean yield,
But leave their symbols in the stunted tree.

We wait until winds clear the moon and see
        The burning oil inside
        A shrine above the tide,
Protected by these dunes out of this sea.

AFTER SAMUEL JOHNSON'S LATIN POEM TO THOMAS LAWRENCE, M.D.[57]

By your life, then, will you confess
Yourself with crude mobs who attack
The wise, who call their power a fake—
Loud braggart fleeing in distress,
Whose only wounds disgrace his back?

You live through evils none ensures
His life against, from which we find
The holy and the brave do not escape.
You have the skill of potent cures,
But miss those purges of your mind.

Throughout the tediousness of night,
Blind opened depths for anything,
Throughout the unworked hours of day,
Cares blot out your paternal sight
And to your core distraction bring.

More than enough of grief at length
Is paid. Raise yourself up from gloom.
You hold the means and know the way.
The healing art, dead sages' strength
Demand from you their life and room.

Sacrifice some human things to God.
Let faith be grace to the tough truss
Of steel men have—do not inveigh.
You bleed on strangest ground unshod.
Come home to your strong mind and us.

AFTER SAMUEL JOHNSON'S *SUMME PATER* [58]

Father most strong, whatever You intend
As to my body's fate—but Jesus, plead—
Do not destroy my mind. Can I offend
In begging life in me for Your own seed?

THE BLOOD OF SHILOH [59]

My father came home from the War too weak
To purge its taint. My brother, a young man,
Survived like some hard thoughtless animal
And never grasped our father's broken mind.
My mother, too, though yet a faithful wife,
Eyed him in ignorance, but hers had scorn—
How could a helpless man work out our life?
Her soul as hardened as her callused hands,
She had turned bitter stoic through the War,
Working to save a threatened farm to keep
The children of her womb from being starved.
For life she killed the woman in her soul.
My father turned to me. At first I thought,
A doting daughter, rest would cure his mind.
Days he seemed himself, but they were brief.
Some fever of the brain seemed stuck in him
That grew in strength when he resisted it,
Some force of slaughter that his gentleness
Never could approve. He strained to fight
It off at night; he could not sleep but kept
One lamp beside his bed, staring for hours
Into its wick, moths thudding on hot glass,
As if he craved to be that piece of cloth
That stayed itself and never flaked in fire.
Only at dawn would sweating sleep dissolve
The demon in his mind, would he have peace.
It was the blood of Shiloh, he once cried,
The waters of Snake Creek that poisoned him.[60]
Wounded in what is called the Hornets' Nest,[61]
A gullied road clotted with Northern guns,
He lay that night out in the storming rains.
Lightning revealed the bodies of the dead,
Their open mouths vomiting out white rain.
And in a sleet at dawn he heard the screams
Of men whose limbs corpsmen were sawing off.

His whole mind broke, its warm interiors
Held by the corpses splattered in the sleet.
The God whom he had loved, a perfect good
Did not survive that slaughterhouse in him.
Reason and faith bled out his inner core.
Only an ingrained discipline, though weak,
Forced him, rote-like, to finish out the war.
It then was worn out. Madness settled in,
And to escape, he came back home and died.
Our body's frame will not bear long a pain
Lodged in the mind—death will seem release.
I prayed for that, out of my love for him.
I feel God's mercy found his godless mind.
He went mad not because a coarsened brain
In him craved evil, for he craved the good
Whose absence his good mind could not endure.

A MEMORY OF THE FRONTIER

Cold wilderness outside, the burning lamp
Beside the bed whereon the old man died
I still can see back of the crowded years,
His white beard yellow in the oily flame.
That winter froze the river; the dogtrot
Whistled in the wind, and still he held
Us in his dying's vise. He broke at last.
The old slave woman who had lived with him
Cleaned the body laid on cooling-boards.
It made me shiver glimpsing water poured
On flesh in that cold time. The women-kin
Tore his bed apart. They took the sheets
Outside and burnt them in the evening fog—
Fire struggled on the clamminess of blood.
The men had had the coffin done by dark.
The neighbors came; huddled at the hearth,
We held a wake, then buried him by noon.

THE HISTORY OF A TRADITIONALIST

He learned what tougher masters can impart,
The salt and muscle of that English art
Before crazed adolescents wrecked its mind.
He took the meat out of the antique rind
And never aped mere manners from the past.
He never fetished tight control. At last
He found the style for plainest naked truth
And in some wisdom bore the end of youth.

And what was his reward in all the lights
Of magazines, rock-stars, and Reaganites,
Of liberal cant about the good, safe id
That only needs the State to screw its lid?
We cannot even say he had one rotten lot.
They absolutely treated him as he was not.

A PRAYER TO THE PARACLETE [63]

God the Spirit, inspire
Our soul's and body's life
With purifying fire.
Let not quick sin be rife.

Cleanse the barren mind
Of crudities and lies
That it, at last, may find
Truth which fructifies.

Let charity fuse whole
The fractured, wounded will,
Each movement of the soul
To God Who makes us still.

And never let despair
Defeat the Father's plan:
Christ gives us God to share
In His shed blood as man.

ON REMBRANDT'S PORTRAIT OF AN OLD MAN READING THE SCRIPTURES [64]

Exposure salted his grave Northern face.
An unerasable sadness tinged that grace
Of sourceless light glowing on solid form.
Hard winter nights—the isolating storm—
His oil burned out onto the living word.
A man matured in loss, in griefs incurred
By love outside himself, he would expend
His mind on God, still opened to the end.

THE AUTOBIOGRAPHY OF A BENEDICTINE [65]

I teach logic to would-be priests,
The subtlest training of the Schools.[66]
A keen, well-bred old hound unleasht,
I track down fallacies of fools.

I read dry Horace, drink wine deep,[67]
Though never yet to drown my wits.
Old Cock is cooked, and so I sleep [68]
Long nights unshaken by his fits.

I feel at ease here on this earth
And love the dogma of God's flesh.
Why should we see a poisonous dearth
In what God still creates afresh?

That sun-struck Porch of Solomon,[69]
Those eunuchs of the maddening groan
Who insult reason, who would stun
Our souls with God, I leave alone.

Athena's grove, its tempered air,[70]
The autumn sun on her olive trees—
I thrive and bead my thankful prayer
To reason's source for clarities.

Our mind is not some Virgil cursed [71]
To go back down to painful shades.
Faith dies itself and is dispersed
In minds the deathless Word pervades.[72]

A PASTORAL OF THE PRIMITIVES [73]

By early June the limbs of the pear tree
Already sag. The weight of its thick fruit
Snaps its joints in just a random breeze,
So rich the womb of meat around the seed!
Sunflowers thrive and blow in deep manure
Where we had kept and fed the fatter bulls
We killed and ate. Noontide is like a god
Who pours himself into the teeming plant
So that we see its essence in white heat.
Only the gross catfish in coffin-vaults
The cows drink water in escape his fire—
They float full-fed on algae and rich scum.
The afternoon expands; the air stays hot.
A bush-hog chews across the pasture just
Below the house, splattered in ironweed.
White egrets swarm for insects in its wake.
The cows stay for that cooler later time
Before they graze, then eat into the night.
They only stop to throw the head of tongue
Over their backs to kill the biting flies,
Leaving coats of spittle on their hides.
Our sight cannot detect the twilight's end
Or night's degrees. Earth fades in black
Extending upwards from the sunken swamp.
Bullfrogs in sexual heat cry desperately
As a full red moon is rising in the east.

SALT FROM THE WINTER SEA [74]

My great-grandmother said each year the men
Would travel to the Gulf—a hundred miles—
To draw salt from the winter sea. They camped
Beside their wagons in the wild sea-oats
And built up fires of lighter-knots and pine.
Black pots boiled for days among the gulls
Upon white dunes, sea-water steaming off
And leaving salt. They sifted out the gross
Impurities. In cool depths of hogsheads
The fusing salt was stored away from heat.
They worked the surf like primitives afraid
Of gulfs, who never sought the sea herself,
Who lived inland and knew the solid earth.
But the last day, after their work was done,
Those stoics lingered in the cloudless calm,
The warm November sun of their Deep South,
The green Gulf crashing on the golden sand.
They momently then gazed outside themselves,
Struck by the mortal beauty of the waves,
Before they packed the salt and started home.

John Finlay, December 1966, age twenty-five, at Grayton Beach, Florida, looking out over the Gulf of Mexico

A Prayer to the Father (1992)[1]

GO LITTLE BOOK [2]

Go little book to the party,
But hide your moral crumb.
Be cunning. Act as if to say,
I'm hungry, Sir, and dumb.

A PRAYER TO THE FATHER [3]

Death is not far from me. At times I crave
The peace I think that it will bring. Be brave,
I tell myself, for soon your pain will cease.
But terror still obtains when our long lease
On life ends at last. Body and soul,
Which fused together should make up one whole,
Suffer deprived as they are wrenched apart.
O God of love and power, hold still my heart
When death, that ancient, awful fact appears;
Preserve my mind from all deranging fears,
And let me offer up my reason free
And where I thought, there see Thee perfectly.

—Spring 1990

THE FAUN [4]

Est-ce en ces nuits sans fonds que tu
　dors et t'exiles?
　　　　　　　–Rimbaud, Le Bateau ivre [5]

He could not sleep. For hours in solitude
He watched his mind in terror at itself
Exhaust his will and burning in its own
Locked speed close in upon itself to dredge
The half-forgotten wreckage of its depths.
The buried images that it tore through
Loosened in the brain's imagined light
As in an atmosphere whose cobalt glare,
Unblinking and cold, absorbed and distantly
Defined the lonely havoc of their drift:
Savannahs rolling in the threaded swarm
Of their own growth lay burning in the slow
Contagion of the sun; again through fog
He saw against their open fires at dusk
The narrow settlements from which he knew
Himself estranged; rejected forms appeared,
Their bodies still abandoned in those nights,
Of women he had forced or gulled into
The brief and awkward void of his lust;
The childhood face of his drowned brother,
Untouched in its reserve and luminous,
Stared helplessly at him as with no mind
Of any choice it sank and was dissolved
In waters held engulfing in his mind.
The gods! The slaughtered herds and images
Drenched in blood! He now saw in his loss
Their far-off purity. No blood nor agony
Compelled that cold archaic peace nor reached
Those distances. The warm unshadowed noons!
The slanting gaps of night!　　　Outside the cave
He glanced across the quiet waste that lay
In cold moonlight for miles below the ridge.
From where he stood he saw at its far edge
The narrow beach that momently undone
Withstood the wide explosions of the tide.
And in that noise he walked until the dawn.

AT KALÁMAI [6]

Bones in cold weeds
are what the sea can know.
All night it waited
outside the house,
you beside me sleeping.
Towards dawn it turned.
The waves crashed
into the cobalt haze,
gave out unto the moon.
They never were enough.
What dream were you turning in
that what I kissed was salt,
lay silent in those sheets?

THE *ILLUMINATION* OF ARTHUR RIMBAUD [7]

African sunlight seared the grimy walls,
The windows opened to the furnace noon.
He gazed into its objectless pure style,
Hermetic light destroying common earth,
Until he saw the fated animal reach night,
This century of holocaust and suicide.

BAUDELAIRE IN BELGIUM [8]

A gradual snow that hides abandoned flesh,
Death engulfs me as the moments pass.
Exhausted mind is ended now, old nag,
For hope leaves it as cold as argument.
The gathering mass will give me in its thaw
A dark and broken thing that costs no pain.
And I? The hooves are bloody from the ride.

STONE AND FIRE

> *L'automne déjà!*
> —Rimbaud, *Une Saison en Enfer* [9]

The wine is drunk more slowly now. It clears
The turgid mind, unbends the wrinkled palm.
Forget, it says, the shives, the rust and smears.
Come take stoic stone, kind colorless balm.

In the slanting gap of night low crickets
Keep at their song in the lean earth and frost.
All night a full moon burns the bare thickets,
The skin of earth, the rivers blind and lost.

FLAUBERT IN EGYPT [10]

He was awakened, for no cause he knew,
To face the brutal moonlight in the room,
Burning the veinless marble of the floor,
Flooding the nameless whore who slept on it.

As if he dreamed, he saw her open mouth,
The painted coins, strung around her throat,
Turned colorless as chalk in the strong light,
The gleaming black skin of her milkless breasts.

He thought of the pearl-fishers diving down
To layered tons of pressure on the skull,
With only shells to answer for the pain—
They surface, bleeding from the eyes and ears.

He dreamed the poem, freed of human act,
A smooth blank thing that turns in nothingness.

A PORTRAIT OF A MODERN ARTIST

The taking years have left her here alone
Out in rough country miles from any town.
Always the victim of the deadly male,
She writes hard fiction, all belief now gone,
And faces fate in nothing but cold style.
She labors on one novel through the years,
A Flaubert fishing by obstinate isles—
With her backwaters of the modern South.
A house lit blue by TV screens at night
Where Man and Woman tear themselves apart
After *he had fucked out her female brains*
Is matter for her art, her *fleurs du mal* [11]
Her characters burn out on sex and drugs.
How clinical she stays, how unconcerned,
As if she would respond to nothing now
But brutal slang and filth that's purified
Of thought, a rotless plastic of the mind.
Why does she strain at trash, compulsively
Work tone and structure right for the insane,
And cut the moral tissue from her soul?
She craves cool surfaces of some black god,
Nietzsche's dry savagery immune to pain
And tests her strange endurance in her art.
With no recoil she sees there moral law
Annulled and dreams chaos come back again,
A world of sex and death shot up on coke.
But during sleep she finds clear limits of
Her tolerance for evil. Sweat breaks out
And her disowned humanity comes through.
Aroused then by the terror of her dreams,
Alone out in the country late at night.
She screams herself awake to stop the fangs
That would tear out her life. Instinctively
She holds to her own form and being's stuff
Against the now felt madness of her art.

THE LOCKED WARDS [12]

Thick walls enclose these women in a tomb.
Blind windows mock the sun that never strikes
Their buried rooms. No season reaches them,
Old and insane, whom only death will find.

The wound will never close. The acid poured
Into their textured souls forever clings
And eats their minds each day. Convulsively,
The need to void the evil claws for life.

One stalks the corridors, clutching torn rags
Against her breast. The disintegrating eye
In the electric glare holds her dead child
Alive each night, whose image burns in sleep.

Jesus, the youngest cries, *You died for us.*
She turns to face them all, then offers blood
Cupped in her rigid palms. Expanding veins
Deny the senseless skull, the hopeless pain.

Inside their cells, the women who have killed
Assume or plead the dead who torture them
Chained to their iron beds. Only near dawn
Do drugs dissolve the brain in sweating sleep.

These walls dissolve. The soul will never be
Absurd, though flayed alive inside this pit.
The madness spawned by loss, the filth of crime
Reveal its naked essence filled with need.

"IF A MAN DRIVE OUT A DEMON . . ." [13]

I know that evil is the absence of a good,
A mind deprived, a truth misunderstood,

A nothing that cannot exist apart
A host, a dark obsession of the heart.

I know, also, existence offers us
In all its forms a way to end the curse.

All this I know, but error follows me
Even to this white page. I live to see

These words, so capable of flesh, become
In me mere fops of concept, wanting scum.

THE END OF THE AFFAIR

I leave now your dank underground small room
Where your lonely cold ego meets its doom.

I lived there lacking objects feeding sense
And vital conflicts, strengthening if tense.

We tried to eat each other's flesh instead
To get at blood which would appease the dead

Who lived on still in us as tragic script.
My bitter reason baulked. It took and ript

My book's mad leaves—I had to turn from you
Conning your hieroglyphs that are not true.

EPIGRAMS AND BRIEFER LYRICS

My friend says epigrams have an easy wit.
He would prefer that twitching bit by bit
Conceit of what he's never sure is it.

All morning at work
The poet is one thought.
Flies crawl and copulate on
His motionless hand.

The benefit of enemies is this:
Identity, too loose and vague in bliss,
Is clenched into a tight emphatic fist.

FOR ALLEN TATE [14]

If now our lean language can sing
Of laurel and the rough dogwood
Caught in the single glow of faith
That led the salty Aeneas to Rome,
It is because of Master Tate.

THE GESTAPO IN THE APARTMENT OF FREUD [15]

What moral force could you command to face
Their brute intrusion in your private place?
Your id is speechless, does not know of death,
Obscured by blood inside its rabid breath.

EPIGRAMS FOR ADVENT [16]

1.

To free us from the dust to dust He came
And made it ashes of the Phoenix flame.

2.

Be patient. The Silent Word unspoken
Moves in all this broken world unbroken.

SKIN FLICKS

The air-conditioning grinding like a fiend
Out-noised the crying bodies on the screen.

THE PIONEERS

The white man aimed his rifle at the head
And waited as the chief approached the house,
Soundless on muffling needles of the pine.
A band of young braves moved behind his back.
They came emerging from those sunken woods
Where one clean spring erupted in a creek.
The white man fired exactly when the chief
Had reached a clearing in the pine and stood
Exposed, a target lit by shafts of light.
The chief fell down convulsive on the ground
And died; his band was struck with terror at
The gun; a panic seized them and they fled.
The whites remained inside the house all day
While buzzards scented in the air the rot
And closed in tighter circles on the corpse.
The night came on in fluid blacker depths,
A shell of hungry forest cats and wolves.
And when the dark was done the dawn revealed
The body of the chief was now just bones.

OFF HIGHWAY 27 [17]

Vines choked off the chimneys
Of the few houses left standing
In those rusted abandoned fields.
Frames froze into the earth.
As windowpanes caught the sun,
Insides burned distantly away.

THE SEASONS OF THE BLOOD

The bulls of deep summer
grazing in thick fields,
wading through gold light . . .
unslaughtered, still alive!

In the fall the old dog
dreams of the bloodied catch.
The winds of the hurricanes
beat against his brain.

These winter stars shine
in depths and nests
of nakedness. We sleep
the long night in blood.

The snake leaves its skin
in the breaking spring—
its wrinkled self nailed
into new earth by rain.

I WILL NOT LET THEE GO [18]

After she fell and broke her hip she stayed
In her back room. Her more than ninety years
Completed her. The yellowed shades were drawn
To cause the coolest dark for her weak eyes.
Her face was indistinct; her flesh collapsed
In those long dewlaps hanging from her arms.
And yet her voice was clear, her words precise.
The massive structure of her bones remained
To make her seem still strong in her old age.
The skin had wasted from the swollen joints
Of her huge hands that hooked like eagle claws
The arms of her wheelchair as she would talk.
"My father cleared us land. That teeming womb
We worked until it gave us our full lives."
Weakness of brain attacked the outer shell
Of present time and killed its just born act.
It left intact her mind's deep core, the past
With sunken roots that only death could pull.

FOR DAVID DURING DARK TIMES [19]

For my sole self, inside myself alone,
Close to a heart, the poem's humid source,
Between a nothingness and pure event,
I wait the echo from my breadth within,
That cistern bitter, grave, and resonant,
Soul's vibrant mold, forever possible!

—from the French of Paul Valéry

Poems from Section V
of *Mind and Blood* (1992) [20]

AT SOME BAR ON LAGUNA BEACH, FLORIDA [21]

Winter, 1969

Outside a night of sleet
That whispers the warp of ice
And low waves that repeat
What always is said again.

Inside a tinted half-light
Blurred the scars of error.
Careful, suspicious insight
Lost its edginess.

Moral strenuousness
Was disarmed by accident
Casual as the hit or miss
Of balls on green baize.

And a defenseless vacancy
Declined into obscurity,
Its thin margin a fantasy
Of surf that shivered onto ice.

THE GRAVES BY THE SEA

A translation of Paul Valéry's *Le Cimetière marin* [22]

This tranquil vault, assuming files of doves,
Is quivering between the pines and tombs.
The perfect noon composes there with fires
The sea, the sea, the always rebegun!
After abstracting thought what recompense
In this long gazing on the calm of gods!

Sacred travail of purest lights consumes
The many diamonds in the sightless foam,
And massive peace bethinks itself alive.
When one sun trusts itself above the void,
The pure effectings of a deathless cause,
Time scintillates, and wisdom is the dream.

The constant hoard, Athena's simple shrine,[23]
Calmness of strength, and visible reserve,
The prideful depths. Eye holding in yourself
So rich a sleep beneath your veils of fire,
Oh my own silence! . . . Building in the soul,
The vault a thousand tiles, heavy with gold!

Temple of time, my essence found in breath,
I climb and use myself to this pure point,
Engulfed inside my vision of the sea.
And for that sovereign gift I owe the gods,
The calm explosion of this light now seeds
A regal scorn in staring down on heights.

Just as fruit melts in our possessing it,
Changing its absence to deliciousness
Inside a mouth in which its form will die,
So here I scent the fumes from my own pyre,
And to the soul consumed the sky intones
The rumors of these seething, changing shores.

That clearest sky observes me too in change.
After astringent pride, after so strange
An idleness, yet filled with pending power,
I now give up myself to burnished space;
Over houses of the dead my future shade
Subdues me to its own gaunt pace on graves.

The soul at solstice naked to its fires,
I am sustaining you, refulgent justice
Of light itself, your shafts so pitiless!
I cede you pure back to your primal place:
Regard yourself! . . . But to reflect the light
Requires that other part of dismal shade.

For my sole self inside myself alone,
Close to a heart, the poem's humid source,
Between a nothingness and pure event,
I wait the echo from my breadth within,
That cistern bitter, grave, and resonant,
Soul's vibrant mold, forever possible!

Do you know, false prisoner of leaves,
Gulf devourer of these slender rails,
On my closed eyes, a secrecy that stuns,
What body drags me to its languid end,
What brow attracts it to a soil of bones?
A spark remembers there my absent ones.

Sacred and closed in bodiless pure fire,
A chthonic fragment sacrificed to light,
This fatal place is pleasing, held by suns,
Composed of gold, of stone, and sombre trees,
Where so much marble trembles over shades—
A faithful ocean sleeping on my tombs!

Shining bitch-hound, keep out idolaters!
When by myself, my peace a shepherd's smile,
I keep and graze the flock, mysterious
White sheep, of all my quiet tombs for hours,
Keep away from here the cautious doves,
The useless dreams, the busy, prying angels!

Once here, the future is an idleness.
Sharp insects cut across the brittleness;
Everything is burnt, destroyed, or shrunk
Into I know not what severe an essence. . . .
Life must be vast, so drunk it is on absence,
And bitterness is sweet, the mind is pure.

The hidden dead fit firmly in this earth,
Which holds them warm to drain their mystery.
The Noon on heights immobile, absolute
There knows itself, agrees with self alone. . . .
Complete pure head, and flawless diadem,
I am the secret, living change in you.

You only have my soul to hold your fears.
My guilt, uncertainties, my blind constraints,
These flaw the water of your perfect stone. . . .
But in their darkness under marble slabs
A people vague among the roots of trees
Have slowly come to seize your primal side.

They have dissolved into thick nothingness.
Red clay drinks our own kind colorless—
Arteries of flowers absorb the given blood.
Where are the dead's unique, quick idioms,
Their arts of being selves, their only souls?
Worms work through where tears were formed.

The sharp cries of girls aroused and felt,
The eyes, the teeth, the eyelids fluid wet,
The maddening breast which teases with desire,
The blood which blazes in the yielding lips,
The final gifts, the fingers guarding them,
All goes to earth, falls back into the game.

And you, proud soul, do you expect some dream
Not stained by all these colors that deceive,
Which sea and gold make here for eyes of flesh?
Will you then sing when you are only air?
My presence now is porous—all must die;
Your sacred restlessness must cease and lie.

Gaunt immortality, gilt-lettered black,
Consolatrix fixed hideously with laurel,
Who transforms death into a mother's breast—
That pious ruse and myth too beautiful,
Who does not know, who yet cannot refuse
The stretched eternal grin, the empty skull.

Father in the depths, unhouseled heads,
Lying beneath that weight of spaded soil,
Who are the earth and who confute our steps,
The true gnawing, the irrefutable worm
Is not for you asleep beneath these slabs—
He lives off life—it's me he never quits!

Love, perhaps, or even hatred of the self?
His secret tooth forms such a part of me
That any name seems right—no matter what!
He sees, feels, dreams, desires and wills!
It is my flesh he likes; even in sleep
I lie transfixed by his unclosing eyes. . . .

Zeno! Cruel Zeno, the Eleatic one! [24]
You cut me with that arrow feathered taut,
Which quivering will fly but never move,
The sound begetting, arrow killing me!
Ah sun, a tortoise shadow for the soul,
Achilles motionless in breathless strides!

But no! . . . Arise! Into successive time!
My body, break apart this pensive mold;
My chest, inhale the naissance of the wind!
A coolness, rising off the breathing sea,
Gives back my soul. . . . Ah salty potency!
Run into waves to reemerge alive!

Yes! Giant sea endowed with ecstasies,
Hide of Bacchic panther, chlamys slit [25]
By thousands of those icons of the sun,
Hydra absolute, drunk in your blue flesh,
Biting endlessly your glittering tail
In noise as deep as silence is its like,

The wind is rising! . . . We must try to live!
Immense air riffles through my taken book;
A reckless wave bursts pulverized on rock.
Let brilliant pages scatter in the flaws!
And crash, waves, crush this tranquil vault
Where crying taut sails plunged, predators!

THE EXILES

In honor of Janet Lewis [26]

1.

The battle took place early fall between
The red men and the whites. But it was brief.
Before the unknown magic of the rifle,
The red men, panic-struck and terrified,
Collapsed and fell apart, and when their chief
Was shot, their power ebbed totally away.
The whole tribe then was rounded up; the old,
The women and the children, all of them,
Uprooted from their land and local god
Were herded west to eke out foreign life.

2.

Time passed, perhaps a week. One afternoon
I felt an eerie crawling on my skin
As when we sense someone unseen close by.
I was outside. I raised my eyes to see
An Indian woman standing in the yard,
Who had been separated from the tribe
And now was wandering in search of it.
A child hung from her back in woven straw.
Her sudden presence startled me; she seemed
Uncanny till I saw she was of flesh.
Warm sunlight cast her shadow on the ground.
She didn't make one sound, but cupped a hand
And raised it to her mouth. I went inside
And brought back food for her, along with milk.
She slowly ate and drank to make them last,
Then swung in front of her the strawed papoose,
And took her child and nursed him on her breast.
She rested there on our porch a little while
And left as silently as she had come.

3.

For some time on the woman lived in me;
I followed her inside my taken mind.
Those nights unsheltered and exposed, the bed
Of leaves on ground too damp and cold by dawn,
The long hard night, the two would have endured
So closely joined I thought of them as one.
I wondered if she found their tribe or if
She and her child were killed by animals or men
So that they lie unburied on wild earth.
The wolves and rattlesnakes she would have faced
Both on the open ground and in the woods.
But if the worst occurred, it was the life
I saw and felt, not death, which stayed with me.
And though some years have passed, I yet can feel
The sunlight of that afternoon in fall
When she consumed the food and fed her child.
I see the exiled pair, the woman's strong
And toughened face, the strangely silent child's
Leaning rearward from his mother's back,
Gazing toward the home he now will never have.

IN THE TIME OF THE CIVIL WAR

I

They were young immigrants, a man and wife,
Who had appeared one day the year before.
They farmed a lot outside our Deep South town
And lived alone but for my father's kindness.
Old men hanged him one morning before church
Out in those water oaks just north of town.
After they lashed the mule drawing the cart
On which he stood, the limb swung down too low
To let the rope cause death. The posse dug
Out with their hands a hole beneath his feet.
But even so, his feet dragged on the ground
As he swung to and fro. He never screamed
Or broke the Sabbath calm of the thick trees.
His unblindfolded eyes, abstract near death,
Were clear in pure despair behind the sweat.
He was their foreigner, his dark skin proof
He spied for Yankees, planted in our South.
And when they left their victim in the flies,
My father cut him down, then dug his grave.
We buried him that day. There were no kin.
The wife, who only spoke their native tongue,
Was near raw madness in my mother's charge.
When she regained her mind, my father took
Her to Mobile from which she sailed for Rome.
It was before the blockade sealed the South.

II

His dreaming mind detached him from the earth.
He lived abstract, as if some sterile knife
Had cut his soul from flesh so that it lived
Unfed with blood; still his eyes were vague,
Not focused on those men and things he saw,
But on some dream of them, in which he sliced
Them from their common nature, their own soil.
My father tried to save his soul; he talked
With him at length and liked the man in spite
Of his strange mind, but never felt he knew
One unchanged self. Man is himself the god

In this new world, he said to Father's shock.
Its virgin land gave the bold man rebirth
If he would wash his mind of the old faiths,
Cross the wild sea, and live in wilderness.
He thought pure nature molded man to good,
Freed from the old God, His kings and popes.
My father said he was afraid of other men,
And even I, still young, yet saw his dreams
Made a shield. I also saw his loneliness—
The dreaming head cut from our mortal heart.

III

Each single man who hanged him died that year
Through violence, the jurist's *acts of God*.
The town still says he haunts the water oaks.
I went there one night seeking him, but found
Just the pure moonlight falling in between
The moving limbs; quick drops of it hit earth
And ran like mercury on the black, hot ground.
His ghost was wilderness, the burning moon.
Through all these years I wonder if he still
Held to his faith at death. The hanging men
Were just the crude, raw pieces of his god.
When he had landed on these shores, that god
Lived on black slaves and was prepared itself
To spill its godhead's blood in fratricide.
Did he have doubts in those white afternoons
Of that harsh light he had not known at Rome?
The human world will not sustain the weight
Of Heaven and man cannot be God's pure self.
I fear at times, though, that another fate
Claimed him the Sunday morning he was hanged.
The posse was white trash, wild lawless men.
As he was being bound and forced from home,
He could have looked into their faces stained
In grime, the unkempt beards and vicious eyes,
And thought he yet saw god, though evil now
And drunk with wrath against the foreign man.

IV

At first the panic fear she would be killed
Unhinged the woman's mind. It took her time
To grasp the fact that she was safe with us.
But troubles of her mind did not then cease.
There was repressed resentment in the wife
Against her husband who had wrenched her from
Their home and taken her to this raw place
Where Christ could not be found in sacrament.
She feared that she was damned in wilderness
And that her husband's soul now suffered hell.
She changed as she resolved to go back home
And when we reached Mobile—the journey then
Took days and I went too—her soul revived
In the old port, its ships, her hope of home.
Although my father balked, I went with her
Inside her church. A long time she confessed.
When she came from the box I watched and saw
She had some peace and was absolved from sin.
In thickening twilight huge bells were rung.
Before we joined my father, she lingered in
The massive dimness of the church and gazed
As candles burned and lit the altar's gold,
Then crossed herself in tears and turned away.
The next day she embarked and left for Rome.

TOLD FROM THE NINETEENTH CENTURY [27]

A blooming vine covered the side front porch
And hid the woman from the strong full moon.
A bird sang in the new-leaved tulip tree,
But Laura did not heed him that spring night.
She was resolved to face her sister's plight.
The state's asylum loomed as the snake pit
Where Mary would be drugged and left to die.
The sister needed constant care. Last week
She wandered to the outskirts of the town,
Descended cliffs and found the river's brink.
She either jumped or fell. A group of boys
Saved her before the currents sucked her in.
The doctor said it was their father's blood,
Diseased by syphilis, that broke her mind.
Her kin, he judged, could only help her now.
The moon burned white, the Artemis who sheds
The animal's warm blood, bloodless herself.
Laura moved her chair, then faced the light.
She would never conceive. Through her void
She would defeat her father's reckless blood,
Ease it to death, though Mary would die too,
In whose decaying brain his sin lived on.
She could not free her soul from bitterness,
But she could save it from the lawless dead.

THROUGH A GLASS DARKLY [28]

My uncle hated Catholics. Through low guile,
And order that would enslave the gaping mind
He said they grasped at Caesar's naked power.
He hated Jews still more. No law or church
Could hold, for him, the wrath or grace of God
Who voids this world to save the private soul.
But yet he craved tight order. He had made,
Between world wars, the Army his own life
Until his drunken brawls got him discharged.
Back home he studied law, but nothing calmed
That violence in him which made him drink.
He wandered in the streets of our small town
Into all hours, unconscious where he fell.
Whiskey inflamed his swollen face, and tears
Ran out his eyes. I somehow got him home.
He couldn't rest there till I read St. Paul
Out loud beneath a harsh and shadeless bulb,
As if the words alone could make him whole.
"Read *that* again," he shouted from the bed.
But sober he was worse. He turned outward
The rage which he, while drunk, inflicted on
A self he thought was damned. Demonic hate
Built up deep painful pressure in his mind.
I was that rotten thing on whom he wreaked
Its strength, unleasht upon an ungrown boy.
He drove me out. I spent those summer nights
On tent-revivals' sawdust floors and heard
Preachers condemn this sinful world to fire,
As if it had been formed not by their God.
Around midnight I crept back to the house,
Went in the back door my mother had unlocked.
His light was burning in his upstairs room.
Those nights I thought him gone, more alien
When sober than when drunk. He was obese.
I looked up the black stairwell; in my mind
He sat there in the heat with no clothes on—
He was the Buddha of white sagging breasts.
I saw the insects crawling on his screens,
The southern night the hell of his own pain.

THE SLAUGHTER OF THE HERD [29]

The trucks will come tomorrow afternoon.
The herd her family had milked for years
Will then be prodded with electric shocks,
Packed and crammed inside the storied trucks
And driven to the auction ring for slaughter.
Her husband's death had brought her to this pass.
For two hard bitter years she tried alone
To run the dairy. Kindness made her fail—
She lacked the harshness to control rough men.
She knew all this but guilt remained; she felt
In selling she betrayed a binding trust.
Sleep was hopeless. She got up from her bed.
Out on the porch, she looked down toward the woods
Below the house. The pasture stretched between.
The herd, she said, would be somewhere down there.
An urge to see the cows for one last time
In their own nature's world gripped hold of her.
Like someone in a dream, she walked across
The lawn and road, then down the sunken lane.
Night had reached its stillest, deepest hour.
A gibbous moon poured water in the west.
The herd was at the lower pasture where
Dense woods in the night-heat breathed out cool air.
She saw a world not man's in speechless calm.
The cattle as they slept or grazed appeared
Like creatures in some myth, whole and primal.
Their bags hung heavy with the morning milk.
She gazed at them in awe until the scene
Of their approaching death then seized her mind.
She heard the thudding blow against the skull.
A pity for the slaughtered creature dying
Ran through her open soul. She suddenly
Saw her death too, for what was left her now
Her husband dead, the herd dispersed and killed?
She looked up at the sky, the gibbous moon
And saw it as a realm of death and cried.

AENEAS IN MODERNITY [30]

We have no chattel gods to make our home;
We have our psyches where we burn and roam.

OF HARRY DUNCAN, BOOKMAKER [31]

He crafts a print and page that gird
The poem's grace and make it manned.
He creates matter for the word,
The *thisness* of the book in hand,
A poem's flesh, its life conferred.

THE SYMPOSIUM FOR SOCRATES

The polished floor mirrors the burning lamps
Well stocked with oil. We guests are purified.
A slave-boy gives us garlands for our heads.
Balsam is passed around; we scent ourselves
With its perfume. Strong wine is disciplined
Through measured water in the mixing-bowls,
But still it brims and flashes glints of fire
By which our brains, recovering their youth,
Will heat themselves in happiness once more.

*

No flute girls shall seduce us at this feast
And make us stupid in their music's power.
We will not bloat our minds on wildest myths
Concerned with early thugs of made-up gods,
Their brutal loves and broils with savages.
The sometimes bitter, sometimes tragic lore
Of these our human lives, wisdom like salt
Which our own minds can gather from the sea,
Shall be tonight the substance of our talk.

Previously Uncollected Poems (2016) [32]

THREE EPIGRAPHS [33]

for an Old Man About to Die, Etc.

Dusk and slow rain invade and erode me.
In this thickening dark what can I be?

The settling dust of death deceives. The tomb
Is as copious as Eve's womb.

Knowing you in hunger and fear,
I walked these hot roads to find you.
Now botched in the head, I am here.
Whom did you want? Who are you?

ADMONITIONS FOR A PERNOCTATION [34]

Do not flee from him to accept
The desperate, teasing dare to fall
Into Narcissus' deep pool
And sink to the blackness of it all.

Where you sluggishly enter a world
Made for your secret evil wish
And your bones and eyes are the prey
To a thousand nibbling fish.

No, rather outstare that grim one
Who stares at you in your bed,
Until tossing and in a cloggy sweat
You curse and wish you were dead.

Never give in to his abstract wish.
He would take you to a land without age,
Where you stare at a mirror of yourself
And strike it in a bloodless rage.

DIALOGUE

"No, please,
I will say no more.
There are no alternatives,
No keys for my locked door.
We have talked this over
Too long: the familiar track
Worn into my brain will only
Lead me to my private rack.
You need your time for others:
The brave reckless souls
Crying in burnt sunlight
Who press for their high goals
In some ecstasy of despair,
Defiant of time and this place,
They will accept nothing
Short of the ultimate breathless grace
Raptured beyond death, beyond life.
I would rather sit in my room
And think of my peculiar wounds.
This rainy gath'ring gloom
Asks nothing of my eyes."

Slowly, evenly the rain came down.
On the roof, down the empty halls
All through the night the sound
Was like a begging patient cry.

INSTRUCTIONS FOR PLANTING A ROSE BUSH

Order old dirt from China-land
And rich compost from Japan.
Plant it in a night haunted by one star.
Around it put a golden circular bar.

Bring water in a silver pot
To nourish our little rose's lot.
Pour it either under a full moon
Or on the point of a shadowless noon.

(Yet any time at all will do
If it to a high fancy be true.)
And emulating as noble hero's deeds
Extirpate fiercely the rank weeds.

Note: To free yourself from the sway
Of nice practicality, in a proud fool's way
Once in a while go ceremoniously insane
Over some beautiful little thing.

OUT IN THE COUNTRY, LATE AT NIGHT[35]

The moon out in the country late at night
Is light, and the cold pale fire of terror.

Possessing, not possessed, it perplexes
Metaphor-making man to a silence.

It is no Diana killing farmers,
Or chasing after the shy shepherd boy.

It is a light and a thing of terror,
Defying explication, cold and pure.

As when we catch an unexpected glance
In the mirror and don't know who we are,

Or wake up near dawn in someone else's house
To hear slow footsteps outside our door,

So then as now we are left in dark places
Where what we know is what we don't, the light.

The moon out in the country late at night
Is light, and the cold pale fire of terror.

A VOYAGE

(for MW, MBP, and JR)

We rowed from the drunken party
Out onto the river as into a thought
Of ourselves as we should be, out under
The absolute order of the thousand stars.

Further and further we went until the sound
Of the party became no louder
Than our oars in the willing water,
And the one or two *plips* of the jumping fish.

Out over the wide river we went
Until the shore became the dark
That is the design of distances
And night and the vigor of our minds,

Moving, seeing things into other things
Until they become most themselves,
As well as revelations of something else—
Both together in the economy of our need.

In that mind we stopped and let the boat drift . . .
How strongly the water cleared of our labor
To bear one by one all the autumn stars,
The water perfectly bearing their ordered fire,

Realizing their circuits even as the river
Moved under them and as we moved
Over the quiet river, our minds guided into
The star-covered water not to rest in it,

But in the Divinity of whom it is a sign:
There, where the justice of His fire
Becomes merciful tears, and still is fire
And still is tears—there we intensely rested,

Like those wise men who came the great space
To kneel at the Lady of dark blue
And worship what she bore, the star-moving Child
Who later would walk the water.

"A WINTER'S TALE" [37]

Lovers in spring are as superfluous
as candles at noontime.

Their proper time is winter when night
descends at five o'clock,

And tree limbs are frozen giant fingers
snapped by howling winds,

And life seems the patient in rigor mortis,
soon ready for the box.

Then the lovers become most themselves:
persistent messengers,

Telling us bitter freezing Thomases
of the coming miracle.

But in the spring they are lost in the wild
Diffusion of their story.

—Palm Sunday, 1964 [38]

A RECOLLECTION FROM CHILDHOOD

Death is like
the cross-eyed boy
from the country
we all knew
back in the lost time
we have lied about.
He always talked
about afterbirth
and wild horses
running in a pasture
late at night.
We did not want
to be seen with him.
But at the end of play
period after we had burned
Indians at the stake,
he came in handy.
He could untie the knots.

NIGHT-PIECE [39]

It is time to go.
Creekwater blackens [40]
In and out of the limbs
Of a fallen oak.
And night is and is not
The blackgreen pine-trees.
For it is too quiet
Now for children,
Quiet as a moccasin [41]
In water.[42]

SONNET 43

Though we undid our nights, we fled the thought
Of the death His crucified gaze bestowed
On us. He made us strangers then who owed
Nothing to what we came back to, yet fought.
That exile wore us down until we sought
Again over the cracked clay the blood-told
Charity—our thin bodies shook in the cold,
Our tightening blood coiled in the skull and caught.

We climbed down to treason. Now the twilight
Attack on memory to spoil again
The hidden springs of fear and to defend
The distorting eye and keep pure its sight.
With slow bourbon we tease oblivion
As night comes down on what we leave undone.

A FUNERAL

When he died a quietness deep and strange
Lay hovering around our humming ears.
His hands still in the folds of the sheet,
His eyes now closed upon some vision
Far past the reckoning of desperate minds.
Was it a home for a lost boy
With everything in place,
The aching hurting paradoxes
Now slain by knights
Like dragons in the fairy tales?
Or perhaps merely the death of life,
The hard iron locks fastened
Around a lead box?
Once he opened his eyes
And looked at us with indulgent contempt,
And smiled at our harassed mortality.
No longer were we his friends,
With this final knowledge in his heart.
After we buried him and heard the clods

Hard and doom-like strike the box,
We ambled back to our frail lives
Feeling restless and left out.
Now we are waiting.

You ask me why so morbid is my wit?[44]
To keep glib fools like you away from it.

2.[45]

Oh Poet Whatchamacallit,
How do your iambs go?
Walt Whitman holds my hand,
God the vertigo!

3.

This tolerant critic hates
Judgement in art and life.
His tolerance must be real.
For proof: look at his wife.[46]

[From "Five Epigrams"]

FROM EPIGRAMS FOR ADVENT [47]

"now in the time of this mortal life"

(The Advent Collect in *The Book of Common Prayer*)

Oh, shadows exist only by the light;
Without the Sun there is formless night.

...

If broken eternity now is Time,
There is a hidden healing in our crime.

THE SIXTIES

Sing a song of syntax,
Belief that's wrenched apart,
Language turned a plaything
To guile the wicked heart.

Sing a song of anguish,
Pascal's hungry cats
Frightened in the alleys
At existential rats.

Sing a song of heresy,
The jitters and the twitch,
The angels plain American
Like every son-of-a-bitch.

Sing a song of smart men
With power in the eye,
Put Mary in a brain-cell
And riddled up the sky.

THIS FALL, THE SOUTH [48]

The western sides of barns stay oven-hot
Where insects glue the tight cocoon of eggs—
Air blowing off the Gulf, the pouring sun!
Fire has cleaned off stubble from the fields.
Late autumn afternoons the children dream
The dead come back. *How can it ever change?*
They ask out in the dust of fervid gold,
The dead, the season fixed inside the soul.

But change will come: under the iron sky
The sleet and ice will seal a frozen earth.
This dawn we pulled a heifer's early calf;
We cleared its nostrils of the viscous film
So it could breathe; the mother's afterbirth
And broken blood lay steaming in the chill.

AFTER BAUDELAIRE [49]

Exhausted mind, once eager for the strife,
Will carry hope no more, whose spurs once pricked
Its headlong flight. Rest then shamelessly,
Old hag. The hooves are bloody from the ride.

The mind is done—for now, tired plunderer,
For love leaves it as cold as argument.
No strength is left the craft of poetry.
No pleasures can revive the useless heart.

And death engulfs me as the moments pass
Like gradual snow that hides abandoned flesh.
I contemplate from heights the dwindling earth
And search no warmth far off in its escape.

The avalanche will leave me in its fall
A dark and broken thing that costs no pain.

THE RETURN [50]

And what do you meet there?
Not ripeness but instead
Unhinged and cornered fear,
Love awkwardly unsaid.

A POEM IN PROSE [51]

Toward sunset the wind lay with a savage dampness.
Nothing broke the silence of the backfields. The
kildees, crying in the distance, only made it stronger.

Along the road, the ditches were matted with dead weeds.
A few stalks of dog-fennel stood, here and there, in the
freezing air. Beyond, the fields stretched away empty
and rust-colored in the cold sunlight.
Vines had covered up the chimneys of the few tenant houses
left standing in them. Their frames were frozen into the
ground and, as the window-panes reflected the setting sun,
the insides of each were burning quietly away.

WORDS FOR A FALL SONG [52]

The wine is drunk more slowly now, and clears
The passioned sight, unbends the wrinkled palm.
Forget, it says, the shives, the rust and smears.
Come take stoic stone, kind colorless balm.

A long shadow a light sound and then lie down

In the slanting gap of night, the crickets
Keep at their song on the lean earth and frost.
All night a full moon burns the bare thickets.
The sleeping lie at rest, and blind and lost.

A long shadow a light sound and then lie down

FOR BABS [53]

Babs, do you know green coolness
Of nights cocooned, thick vines of wisteria,
A hive vibrant with crickets and summer insects?
The train is oil lamps across water. . . .
A full savage moon rises in myth.
All emblems of the South burn in a night
Eddying in blackwater, disinterested fires.

Additional Poems, Versions of Poems,
Fragments, Lines, and Related Writings
from the Diaries and Other Sources [54]

ODE TO POETRY [55]

Thou sweet poetry which floest from above,
Fill me with serene thoughts and tender love.
Guider of my soft and tender musing,
Kind and faithful friend, remain ever to my using!

From *The Blue Record Diary*, 1967–72

The Thames a tired god

The shadows of the city lengthen out
To shade by slow degrees of oil and trash

The Thames, tired god, along whose banks no fire

JF Miscellaneous Prose and Diary Entries Folder

FAREWELL TO THE SOUTH

I knew your thickened nights,
The Gulf below us warm
The fireflies' constant swarm

Inside the house felt the past
The demoned father claimed my flesh

the walls seemed opened up

My walls behind   My room seemed opened up in space

AT SOME BAR ON LAGUNA BEACH, FLORIDA, WINTER 1969

Outside a night of sleet
That whispers the warp of ice / whispering
And low waves that repeat
What always is said again.

Inside a tinted half-light
Blurred the scars of error.
Careful, suspicious insight
Lost its edginess.

Moral strenuousness
Was disarmed by accident
Casual as the hit or miss
Of balls on green baize.

And a defenseless vacancy
Declined into obscurity,
Its thin margin a fantasy
Of surf, sublunary and tranced.

Crumbling in the moon.[56]

Another stanza [57]

To know the flesh, the warm muscular night

The source that takes and yet gets taken from.

. . .

I dreamed I saw a picture of myself [58]
As one I could have been, now years ago.

. . .

At first I thought I recognized the face,
A friend (Someone) forgotten now I had half known
In childhood

For James on Beginning the Book

All morning at work
The poet has one thought—
Flies crawl and copulate on
His motionless hand.

CORFU [59]

The leaves of the olive trees are a dull green.
When the wind overturns their undersides
it looks like a school of small gray fish
trying to swim against the current.

a life that took and yet got taken from

. . .

[NOTES FOR POSSIBLE POEMS]

the pool halls
the water-tanks grotesque in the moonlight or silver
    or like an obese primitive idol or god
the filling station
the street lamps with their galaxies of insects
the windows spattered with insects
the narrow roads
the fields
the churchyards, their grave-yards
the houses with their one lonely night-light burning
    in the halls, their roofs covered with moonlight like snow

---

The Red Three-in-One-Notebook

The dead, the living are together there.

The truthful going in the mind; the truthful working of the mind

. . .

The hard detail. Think a long time about it.

—The rain across the branch.
—The snakes in autumn, the mates finding the killed one.
—After the beach and going after Red.
—The oats and wheat.
—The hurricanes and the dream.

. . .

IN MEMORY OF WILLIAM FAULKNER, DIED JULY 1962 [60]

He died in midst of a hot summer—
The land parched and dried, waiting for rain
And the heat-waves dancing drunkenedly
Over the earth that still carried its curse
(Like a packet of old, dirty letters
Containing the ageless threats.)
His home, his land for a moment
Paid tributes on the radios and television
Interspersed with notices of bomb-explosions
Ripping up the bowels of the earth,
And promised tax reductions.
The artist in his death finding
Room among the meaningless rabble.
When we heard it, we felt a ~~pain~~ panic—
~~The pain one feels when the army~~
Suddenly realizing how few we are,
With the senseless night full of
Idiotic laughter forced from ~~desperate~~ sick lungs,
Stealing upon us, engulfing us.
~~With universal death~~
We need our artists. Among the
Yelping and howling of hungry wolfs [*sic*],
They weave the magic web of thought
And remind us of things likely forgotten
In times of hunger and evils—
The old verities of the human heart.

from Epigrams for Advent

Though faintly up from dark woods, yet their cries
Mount interstellar space still as sighs.

I WILL NOT LET THEE GO

After she fell and broke her hip she stayed
In her back room. Her more than ninety years
Completed her. The yellowed shades were drawn
To cause the coolest dark for her weak eyes.
Her face was indistinct; her flesh collapsed
In those long dewlaps hanging from her arms.
And yet her voice was clear, her words precise.
The massive structure of her bones remained
To make her seem still strong in her old age.
The skin had wasted from the swollen joints
Of her huge hands that hooked like eagle claws
The arms of her wheelchair as she would talk.
Weakness of brain attacked the outer shell
Of present time and killed its just born act.
It left intact her mind's deep core, the past
With sunken roots that only death could pull.

―――

"My father cleared us land. That teeming womb
We worked until it (she) gave us our full lives." [61]

―――

I.[62]

And so the year comes grinding to its end
Along the ashen heaps of used-up hopes
And tangled dreams that round us cast their ropes
Of subtle steel which is the power of sin.
Nothing can please us here: all that has been
Our little good becomes the crafty dope
To lull our mind to sleep and wash and soap
Our dirty selves that turn and burn and rend.

Oh, change your wicked ways. Get from bed.
Grade your papers, sir, and mend your ways.
There's a hot hell waiting for lazy men
Who lie in bed and dream just like the dead.
Oh you do not there want to end your days.
Work! Work! and be the Good Lord's little friend.

A POEM IN PROSE [63]

Toward sunset the wind had lain down into a clinging dampness. Nothing alive broke the silence of the back fields—the kildees crying made it stronger. Along the road, the ditches lay matted with dead weeds. A few stalks of dog-fennel stood, here and there, in the freezing air. Beyond, the fields stretched away empty and rusted-colored in the cold sunlight. Vines had covered the chimneys of the few tenant houses left standing in them. Their frames were frozen into the ground and as the windowpanes reflected the setting sun the insides of each were burning quietly away.

From *The Green Corfu Diary* (1972)

Above our minds the alien stars

. . .

I live on   You are someone else

Our island nights are stars,
Dried fields of crickets

The human act defined.

. . .

Those island nights were buried   / sunk
Like crickets in summer grass

      The mind is cleared.

. . .

An old stranger

. . .

The wasp on the head of a snake

The wasp on a snake's head
That coiled within our skulls / ~~That was caught~~

. . .

My last night here

No more this island filled
With strange noises

                        Those deep fields of silence

Last night we walked half way up the mountains of Pelekas[64]

Deep summer nights   Remember

Summer nights on that island
We walked half-naked

Summer nights on islands

Summer nights on that island
We climbed Pelekas

Remember those island nights
We climbed Pelekas

. . .

Last night I dreamed myself as someone else.[65]

In dreams I see a faded photograph
Wrinkled by many hands.

It was myself as once I could have been.
                        I could have been that child.

The childhood face of his drowned brother
Untouched in its reserve and luminous
Stared helplessly at him as with no mind
Of any choice it sank and was dissolved
In seas that lay engulfing in his mind.

. . .

I drank one beer
  There is nothing here

. . .

Sasanquas blooming in Sabbath sunshine [66]
The far-off South. All afternoon it took
Those clouds to pass the sky, huge thunderheads.

From *The Green Paris Diary* (1973)

Staring into the grave, against all odds,[67]
They in their turn fight back convulsively.

Convulsed before the grave, against all odds

Against all odds, staring into their graves
They yet fight back convulsively the void.

And though their bodies break beneath the strain
They still fight back convulsively the void.

The evil that brutal men had done to them,
The past alive, eats out their minds each day—

And yet, against all odds, they still resist

From *The No. S 11712 Notebook* (the 1980s)

The poem about Athena & Orestes:[68]
The soft resistless smoothness of inside
(The human mind, self, body, guts, etc.)
Where no barrier of skull (or like the skull)
Can give out, defend us against, the inroads, etc.

The loneliness of the wanderer. the isolated, rural,
rustle, provincial, narrow-minded, mean country

A law unto your lawless kind

No god can (or will) match the fury of the self

No restraints exist inside to prevent the excesses of
self-destruction, especially when one feels that the
god himself has ordered the execution.
I arose not from, the matrix of the mother-land
But in the colonies.

The ancient matrix of the mother-land
didn't see my birth (know, experience, cause).

Adjectives about "colonies": new, cosmopolitan. deracinated,
rootless, exposed, bewildering, dense, barbaric, unconventual [69]

unfenced

Did some crisis with barbaric Asia
Instigate my sudden, inexplicable birth?

How do the Erinyes actually look? Hogs covered [70]
with clotted blood and filth? Too much?

Read again *Oedipus at Colonus* for description of Athens.[71]
as well as concluding part of *The Eumenides*[72]
No justice informs the torture you inflict.

Poems from the Greek [73]

p. 179 in Fränkel – the Sappho poem [74]

Cool water of the spring air
ripples through apple leaves

the Archilochus poem: I too can lead the dithyramb[75]

We left the molded corpse (fed blood in tubes), the grave[76]
of our father . . . the steatopygous female fertility
dolls holding, clutching the eternal breast, staring blankly
with single-minded fanaticism, single-minded intensity
the painted dolls, steatopygous solidity
Our god is male, unrooted Zeus

the bastards, younger men (merchants, traders, [pirates]

the huddled villages

Ionian seaside towns

Did our existence seem so tentative on the littoral of Asia
                                        on the islands off
barbaric Asia
that we sought comfort in a <deathless / No cause>?

Truth is truth whether it is found outside something or inside
something.

From *The Orange Journal* [77]

Obscure disasters and in colorless balm [78]
Obscure disasters, and the end kind / the balm

. . .

In the slanting gaps of night, the crickets [79]
Keep at their song on the lean earth and frost.
A red moon burns through the bare thickets.
In sleep we lie content and blind and lost.
Obscure disasters end in colorless balm.

. . .

the last part: merely to be considered [80]

the woman who thought or says she is God

Go through all of this very carefully, before you get it
(or any of it) on paper. The great danger is a superficial simplicity
with no echoes or resonance to it.

God is dead – God has been murdered – God has died some kind of
natural death like cancer – God is dying – *the universe is his dying body*
– the universe goes down to death as God's heart gives out

The effect of God's death:

on the universe (what words would a country woman, a blunt, plain-
spoken Anglo-Saxon use to describe this?) Beside universe: the world,
the sky, the heavens, the earth, all of life, the space, the cosmos,
infinity, creation, "the heavens and the earth," "and the world was
without form"

(All space warped and plunging into a cancerous silence or void)

A prison, a hospital, the plague, disease[,] vermin, hanging, burning,
fire.

? And one, too quiet for the rest, whose voice is soft.

. . . that for her creates the world
a movement that for her creates the world
pattern

the other one is dying or has died

And one who cannot walk.

Whose death compels her to his work

the whole extent of space would fall, collapse, disintegrate

whose mind holds space and conserves all life
                                  and spasmatic, trembling
her hands, the veins, expanded

she makes (making) with her hands the veins . . .
a movement . . .
is sweat too much?

she moves her hands over the paralyzed legs

Her body bent over . . . No, it was straight upright

she sits beneath a window that catches
the sunlight and only in it . . . .

the sunlight gleams, burns, gilds, strikes
illuminates the bars, the walls, her face,
        her eyes . . . her hands

Others may ask of hate the numbness
of stones, the cold waters of thin suspended weeds
that do not float on tidelessness.

Others may ask of hate the mask that
calcifies the warm flesh, leaving her
settled ash, derisions, scorns too distant for hate

Others may be of absences, a bed hollowed
by some god whose distances creeds dogmas

Others may burn through, and at the end

Others may burn out hate and in its ash

Others may burn through hate and in its ash

Others disperse themselves in hate

the body, the frame, the bones, the flesh

Because their bodies tremble at the shock
                               cannot take

Because their flesh cannot sustain the shock
weak and frail

tired   fragile

worn   exhausted

wearied   finished

broken   slender

Because their flesh no more absorbs the shock

Because their frames cannot sustain the shock
                                        flesh

Because their flesh cannot support the strain

Because their flesh no more absorbs the strain

With nothing left to break its lonely speed

With nothing to distract

In space held expanding in the skull

With speed caught quickening in the skull

Because their bodies now are lame and frail

The awful longing for existence burns

   . . . the power of the acid drop—the power of the hammer

From *The Baton Rouge Diary*
(June–October 1980)

June 16, 1980.

Omission is the beginning of all art. Lytton Strachey.

What does one omit? The nitpicking, academic detail, the unimportant fact that clutters and obscures.

TO ST. LUCY [81]

Lady, in this northern night
Your past light still threads
Samite-like the present pall
If only in memory
Tired in time and your delay.
Lady, the ignomies
That I have done
In that long time
Since you last came to me!
Your light is now my shame
Now that I know you when I am
Where you are not.
And yet the strange praise
This ice and midnight offer you,
Blind Lady of light!

Once at the kind solstice
You held me lightsome
In so pleasing a grace
My mind, then close to its desire,
Consented to the ancient pun . . . .
I would have died for you,

Lady, decorous of grace!
That pastoral courtesy
Remembered in barrenness
Promises even till now
The threads your sight
Will weave into gold
What now is broken in this cold.

TOLD FROM THE NINETEENTH CENTURY [82]

A blooming vine covered the side front porch
And hid the woman from the strong full moon.
A bird sang in the new-leaved tulip tree,
But Laura did not hear him that spring night.
She was resolved to face her sister's plight.
The state's asylum gaped like a snake pit
Where Mary would be drugged and left to die.
The sister needed constant care. She lost
Herself beside the river; from the boulder
She either jumped or slipped. A group of boys
Saved her before the current sucked her in.
It was their father's blood, the doctor said,
Diseased by syphilis which broke her mind.
Her kin, he judged, could only help her now.
Laura moved her chair and faced the moon.
She would never marry James who wrote that week
And forced a choice between himself and Mary—
I will not let stark madness in our house.
There were no other kin. For Mary's sake
She would give up her life. Refusing James,
She would annul their father's lawless blood
And end the line. But Mary yet still lived,
In whose decaying brain his sin returned,
The sister whom she loved and could not leave.

THE LAST ACT [83]

> *'Tis the god Hercules whom Antony*
> *Loved now leaves him.*

It is too often only close to death
Or utter failure, when the mind is held
To truth, we see the outlines of the gods,
Those whom we loved but never realized.
Above us in a void burnt-out and cold,
At unfamiliar heights their forms return
Ghostly and move across the final night,
Remote and unappeased in our collapse.
There is no bitterness in facing them.
The heart that fatally kept them deprived,
And saw them hostile to the living blood
Will pay in blood its error, every vein.
In what is not the gods are reconfirmed,
The candor of their presence briefly seen.
The tragedy leaves nothing else but that.
Then they are gone. The music underground,
The quiet terror of its shifting source,
Its echoes vanishing, is all that's left.

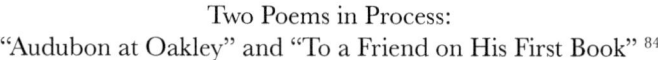

Two Poems in Process:
"Audubon at Oakley" and "To a Friend on His First Book" [84]

AUDUBON AT OAKLEY [85]

My Gallic cunning poured sweet wine into
The calyxes of trumpet-vines and caught
Small drunken birds a bullet blows apart.
Others I shot, pinned them to a board
To draw the fresh-killed life. Elusively,
The *is* that quickens in the living eye
Escaped the sweat of art, and drying ink.[86]

I tore blind pages till I reached the one
That pleased my avid mind. The wilderness

There teems with birds I never saw before;
White and wood ibises, the sparrow hawk,
The red-cock woodpecker, and painted finch.
I hunted them for days and nights until
I throve in timelessness. One day stood out.

The fall was blazing in the silent trees; [87]
~~Wedges of geese were passing overhead.~~ [88]
I heard below all things the river sough.
I saw my book, taut wings of mockingbirds
In combat with the snake knotted beneath
The nest its open mouth close to the eggs,
Now held forever in the lean, hard line.
And underneath, defining them, combined:
The clean abstraction of their Latin names,[89]
The vulgate richness of this Saxon salt.[90]

TO A FRIEND ON HIS FIRST BOOK [91]

How strange seeing your poems in a book.
I once could feel the pathos of those nights
About them still in hottest Baton Rouge,
Black coffee, poverty, the sweated line!
They only are themselves in this rich book.[92]
I read them as a stranger, not a friend—
Poems get deathless, out of our control—
And see the man who started them consumed.[93]

THE DEAD [94]

Where nothing can be other than it was,
I saw the house still vivid in my mind,
And for years after it had been destroyed.
It stood in sycamore, live-oak and pine,
Seasons drenching still its solid frame.

Sasanquas thriving in the winter sun,
Cool air inside like water from a well
As summers scorched and flaked away old paint,
Fall rains sounding in the rooms all night—
These laved and filled the backward mind.

I saw the family still gathered there,
In light that thickens in the wilderness—
The upper columns seethed in summer bees—
And knew the past encoded in the blood
As deaths perfected it and sealed it up.

I swept away the clotted leaves and dirt
From graves my uncle took me out to clean.
The early autumns drunk with their own seed
When, breathing warmest air, I felt the tongue
Of the cold slab engulf our vulgate name.

She who last lived there finally alone
Died terrified, flesh holding on to flesh.
There were no tears when agony had ceased.
We closed her eyes, transfixed in nothingness.
Then left her covered in the naked light.

I left the house. The sun was rising keen
In burning fog away from each hard leaf.
A swimmer coming out of blinding salt,
I stared where trees stood rooted in a world
Brutal and calming in the clearing sun.

The American Tragedies:
A Chronology of Six Poems
(1987)[1]

THE COOLING-BOARDS

Cold wilderness outside, the burning lamp
Beside the bed whereon the old man dies
I still can see back of the crowded years,
His white beard yellow in the oily flame.
That winter froze the river; the dog-trot
Whistled in the wind, and still he held
Us in his dying's vise. He broke at last.
The old slave woman who had lived with him
Cleaned the body laid on cooling-boards.
It made me shiver glimpsing water poured
On flesh in that cold time. The women-kin
Tore his bed apart. They took the sheets
Outside and burnt them in the evening fog—
Fire struggled on the clamminess of blood.
The men had had the coffin done by dark.
The neighbors came; huddled at the hearth,
We held a wake, then buried him by noon.

THE PIONEERS

The white man aimed his rifle at the head
And waited as the chief approached the house,
Soundless on muffling needles of the pine.
A band of young braves moved behind his back.
They came emerging from those sunken woods
Where one clean spring erupted in a creek.
The white man fired exactly when the chief
Had reached a clearing in the pine and stood
Exposed, a target lit by shafts of light.
The chief fell down convulsive on the ground
And died; his band was struck with terror at
The gun; a panic seized them and they fled.
The whites remained inside the house all day
While buzzards scented in the air the rot
And closed in tighter circles on the corpse.
The night came on in fluid blacker depths,
A shell of hungry forest cats and wolves.
And when the dark was done the dawn revealed
The body of the chief was now just bones.

ELEGIES FOR THE IMMIGRANTS

They hanged him Sunday morning before church
Out in those water-oaks just south of town.
After they lashed the mule drawing the cart
On which he stood, the limb swung down too low
To let the rope bring death. The old men dug
Out with their hands a hole beneath his feet.
But even so, his feet dragged on the ground
As he swung back and forth. He never screamed.
His unblindfolded eyes, abstract near death,
Were clear in pure despair behind the sweat.
My father, who had tried to stop the murder,
Was nearly killed himself; the old men's rage
Despised the man of God, his reasoned plea
That the doomed man had not committed crime.
He was their *foreigner,* his dark skin proof
He spied for Yankees, planted in the South.
And when they left their victim in the flies,
My father cut him down, then dug his grave.
We buried him that day. There were no kin.
The wife, who only spoke their native tongue,
Was near raw madness in my mother's charge.
We had no way of breaking through her fear
She would be murdered too in our strange land.
When she regained her mind, my father took
Her to Mobile from which she sailed for Rome—
It was before the blockade sealed the South.

His dreaming mind detached him from the earth.
He lived abstract, as if some sterile knife
Had cut his soul from flesh so that it moved
Unfed with blood; still his eyes were vague,
Not focused on those men and things he saw,
But on his dream of them, in which he sliced
Them from their common nature, their own self.

My father tried to save his soul; he talked
With him at length and liked the man in spite
Of his strange mind, but never felt he knew
One unchanged self. Man is himself the god

In this new world, he said to Father's shock.
Its virgin soil gave the bold man rebirth
If he would clean his mind of the old faiths,
Cross the wild sea, and live in wilderness—
Pure nature shaped the human stuff to gods
So that all men could live as brothers here.
My father thought he was afraid of other men,
And even I, still young, yet saw his theory
Made a shield. I also saw his loneliness—
The dreaming head cut from our mortal heart.

The town still says he haunts the water-oaks.
I went there one night seeking him, but found
Just the pure moonlight falling in between
The moving limbs; quick drops of it hit earth
And ran like mercury on the black, hot ground.
His ghost was wilderness, the burning moon.
When he had landed on these shores he found
His god lived on black slaves and was prepared
To spill its godhead's blood in fratricide.
Did he have doubts in those white afternoons
Of that harsh sun he had not known at Rome?
The human world will not sustain the weight
Of heaven, and man cannot be God's own self.
They crack in tension; tragic truth ensues.
I fear at times, though, that another fate
Claimed him the Sunday morning he was hanged.
The posse was white trash, old lawless men.
As he was being bound and forced from home,
He could have looked into their vicious eyes
And thought he yet saw God, though evil now
And drunk with wrath against the foreign man.

At first the panic fear she would be killed
Unhinged the woman's mind. It took her time
To grasp the fact that she was safe with us.
But troubles of the mind did not then cease.
There was repressed resentment in the wife
Against her husband who had wrenched her from
Their home and taken her to this raw place
Where Christ could not be found in sacrament.

She feared that she was damned in accident
And that her husband's soul now suffered hell.
She changed as she resolved to go back home
And when we reached Mobile—the journey then
Took days and I went too—her soul revived
In the old port, its ships and hope of home.
Although my father balked, I went with her
Inside her church. A long time she confessed.
When she came from the box I looked and saw
She had some peace and was absolved of guilt.
Twilight descended now; huge bells were tolled.
Before we joined my father, she lingered in
The growing dimness of the church and gazed
As candles burned and lit the altar's gold,
Then crossed herself in tears and turned away.
The next day she embarked and left for Rome.

THE BLOOD OF SHILOH

My father came home from the War too weak
To purge its taint. My brother, a young man,
Survived like some hard thoughtless animal
And never grasped our father's broken mind.
My mother, too, though yet a faithful wife,
Eyed him in ignorance, but hers had scorn—
How could a helpless man work out our life?
Her soul as hardened as her callused hands,
She had turned bitter stoic through the War,
Working to save a threatened farm to keep
The children of her womb from being starved.
For life she killed the woman in her soul.
My father turned to me. At first I thought,
A doting daughter, rest would cure his mind.
Days he seemed himself, but they were brief.
Some fever of the brain seemed stuck in him
That grew in strength when he resisted it,
Some force of slaughter that his gentleness
Never could approve. He strained to fight
It off at night; he could not sleep but kept
One lamp beside his bed, staring for hours
Into its wick, moths thudding on hot glass,
As if he craved to be that piece of cloth
That stayed itself and never flaked in fire.
Only at dawn would sweating sleep dissolve
The demon in his mind, would he have peace.
It was the blood of Shiloh, he once cried,
The waters of Snake Creek that poisoned him.
Wounded in what is called the Hornets' Nest,
A gullied road clotted with Northern guns,
He lay that night out in the storming rains.
Lightning revealed the bodies of the dead,
Their open mouths vomiting out white rain.

And in a sleet at dawn he heard the screams
Of men whose limbs medics were sawing off.
His whole mind broke, its warm interiors
Held by the corpses splattered in the sleet.
The God whom he had loved, a perfect good,
Did not survive that slaughterhouse in him.
Reason and faith bled out his inner core.
Only an ingrained discipline, though weak,
Forced him rote-like to finish out the war.
It then was worn out. Madness settled in
And to escape, he came back home and died.
Our body's frame will not bear long a pain
Lodged in the mind—death will seem release.
I prayed for that, out of my love for him.
I feel God's mercy found his godless mind.
He went mad not because a coarsened brain
In him craved evil, for he craved the good
Whose absence his good mind could not endure.

TOLD FROM THE NINETEENTH CENTURY

A blooming vine covered the side front porch
And hid the woman from the strong full moon.
A bird sang in the new-leaved tulip tree
But Laura did not hear him that spring night.
She was resolved to face her sister's plight.
The state asylum gaped like a snake pit
Where Mary would be drugged and left to die.
The sister needed constant care. She lost
Herself beside the river; from the boulder
She either jumped or slipped. A group of boys
Saved her before the current sucked her in.
It was their father's blood, the doctor said,
Diseased by syphilis which broke her mind.
Her kin, he judged, could only help her now.
Laura moved her chair and faced the moon.
She would not marry James who wrote that week
And forced a choice between himself and Mary—
I will not let stark madness in our house.
There were no other kin. For Mary's sake
She would give up her life. Refusing James,
She would annul their father's lawless blood
And end the line. But Mary yet still lived,
In whose decaying brain his sin returned,
The sister whom she loved and could not leave.

THROUGH A GLASS DARKLY

My uncle hated Catholics. Through low guile,
Strict order that enslaves the gaping mind,
He said they grasped at Caesar's naked power.
He hated Jews still more. No law or church
Could hold, for him, the wrath or grace of God
Who kills this world in His descent to us.
And yet he craved tight order. He had made,
Between world wars, the Army his own life
Until his drunken brawls got him discharged.
Back home he studied law, but could not calm
That violence in him which made him drink.
He wandered in the streets of our small town
Into all hours and slept where he fell down.
Whiskey enflamed his swollen face, and tears
Ran out his eyes. I somehow got him home.
He couldn't rest there till I read St. Paul
Out loud beneath a harsh and shadeless bulb,
As if the Word alone could make him whole—
He used chaos of drugs to prove its grace.
"Read *that* again," he shouted from the bed.
But sober he was worse. He turned outward
The rage which he, while drunk, inflicted on
A self he thought was lost. Demonic hate
Built up deep painful pressure in his mind.
I was the rotten thing on whom he wrecked
Its strength, unleashed upon an ungrown boy.
He drove me out; I spent the summer nights
On tent-revivals' sawdust floors and heard
Wild men condemn this sinful world to fire,
As if it had been formed not by their God.
Around midnight I crept back to the house,
Went in the back door my mother had unlocked.
His light was burning in his upstairs room.
Those times he seemed enshrined, more alien
When sober than when drunk. He was obese.
I looked up the black stairwell; in my mind
I saw him in his chair with no clothes on
Beside the window, holding some dark text.
He looked like Buddha of the sagging breasts
And stared transfixed in his inhuman calm.

Appendices

Appendix A

Notes for the Perfect Poem by John Finlay [1]

1. It must be about the truth. It must give truth.

2. It must be literal, very literal.

3. It must be symbolic, very symbolic, but symbolic only in terms of its literal "base" or narrative, not in terms not growing out of this literal whatever you may call it.

4. It must be literal, very literal.

5. It must be clean and lean and have the supple, yet firm movement of pure muscle.

6. It must be of the physical world, have winter mornings, summer nights, stripped trees, creeks, smoke, smells, the reflection of a star in a bucket of water, etc. in it so that the reader will say, "Oh, yes, this is just the way it really is."

7. Yet it must also be abstract.

8. It must come from a man who is mature and has mastered himself so that he is calm in the good knowledge he has of our mystery, our language and history.

9. It must be rooted in a particular place.

10. It must be whole in its beautifully compelling demand that its reader engage his wholeness, both his intellect and his emotion.

11. It must be moral and cause the reader to make one of the three following statements: "I should and want to lead that kind of life." "I should not and do not want to lead that kind of life." "I should and want to have the patience to resign myself to these unavoidable facts about life."

12. It must have both the intensity of engagement and the detachment of judgment.

13. It must be fully realized in language.

14. It must be plain.

Appendix B

The Mary Roberts Rinehart Foundation Proposal by John Finlay [1]

The project I have in mind is a book of poems. Half of it will be made up of short poems, more than half of which has already been completed. The other will be a long poem, half-narrative, half-meditative, on the life of the artist-naturalist John James Audubon, limited to the Southern phase of his career. The rest of the short poems I can finish on my own, what with various part-time jobs I hold to. It is on account of the long poem that I am asking for your assistance. It will require two or three months of sustained work, including extensive readings in the literature on Audubon beyond what I have already done, some limited travel in Louisiana, particularly Baton Rouge, where a great number of the original prints are located, and St. Francisville, where he lived and worked during most of his stay in Louisiana, and, finally, the actual composition itself. I do not see at present how it will be possible for me even to begin it without a period of financial independence.

Before I give a synopsis of the project, let me make one or two general comments on the poem. First of all, I do not intend for it to be a loose, vaguely subjective account of this cunning, single-minded Frenchman. I hope that it will be rooted in history and fact, and evolve from actual observation of Audubon's wilderness, or the little that is left of it today. This does not mean that it will be unpoetic. For me the greatest poetry comes, not from fantasy, but from intense, realistic perceptions of the natural and human worlds. Secondly, the form will be that of traditional blank verse, but with enough variations to keep it from predictability.

The theme is the immersion of Audubon's mind and art in the American wilderness of the 19th century, his recovery from it, and then the discipline and passion necessary to understand the experience and translate its beauty into art. Audubon is the prototype of the artist, who has to shift back and forth between two sometimes conflicting worlds: the experience of the wilderness, immediate, sensual, nonintellectual, and the mental state of detachment from that experience, in which the mind works through the wilderness into art. This often results in irony, and the central one in Audubon's life is that he has to kill the bird first before he can give it life in art. Apart from this, I hope to get across in the poem the simple fact of the American landscape, its vastness and compelling beauty.

The poem will be in three parts. The first section is the "night journey," the artist leaving the security of a protected life to go on a journey, the end of which is the realization of his art. On the narrative level, this first part is concerned with the boat trip down the Mississippi, which Audubon took at the beginning of his career, in 1820, after having left his family behind, who planned to join him later. His destination is first New Orleans, and, afterwards, St. Francisville, where the vision of his life's work really began to come into focus: *The Birds of America*, the monumental work later published in London. I hope to get across the whole sense of the river and the frontier life along its banks, which Audubon observes and applies to himself:

>   . . . through fog
> He saw against the open fires at dusk
> The narrow settlements from which he knows
> Himself estranged . . .[2]

The boat is comprised of the kind of motley group that usually made up frontier boats of the time: ruffians, drifters, and con men, all of whom are contrasted with Audubon, a figure held together by will and purpose.

The second part will deal with his experiences in New Orleans. On the symbolic level, we have, in this section, the various kinds of temptations which the artist must first overcome before he can seriously begin his work. As in mythical contexts, the artist must first strip and cleanse himself before he can enter the sacred grove. In Audubon's case, this involves freeing himself from distractions, extricating himself from a confusing social scene, and clearing his mind of anything that would interfere with his art and his work in the wilderness. In my poem, this is what Audubon does in New Orleans. Against the background of a varied, colorful, but often violent swarm of life, which the port city was, Audubon attempts to make a living as a portrait painter. He gives it up, finally, after having decided that it is a compromise and an irrelevance to the main purpose of his life. The central figure of this part of the poem is the mysterious "nude" lady, whose portrait Audubon painted. He tells us in his *Journals* that his hands trembled as he held the brush, and he had to force himself to concentrate on the canvas. He interprets her as a kind of temptation, a Southern Circe[3], a beguiling gaze animated by secret beauty. But to give in to her would also be surrendering to a society decadent and artificial. He then leaves for St. Francisville and the woods around it, all swarming with life.

The last part will be much the longest and broadest in scope. It takes place primarily at Oakley Plantation, near St. Francisville, though it will cover other areas of the South that Audubon lived and worked in. Here he realizes his art and makes his first really significant breakthrough. I plan to incorporate the many fascinating details, found in the *Journals*, concerned with the Louisiana wildlife and landscape. We see him in his semi-intuitive, semi-intellectual contact with the raw, even primitive, aspects of the wilderness, and observe the cunning and craft he used to get his prey and then to reproduce the almost inexplicable mystery of its livingness, the actual look in the mockingbird's eye as it hovers in the air, poised, its wings outspread, ready to fight the rattlesnake coiled tightly around its nest.

Finally, it is very difficult to talk about a poem that one wants to write, but which exists in the necessarily vague state it has before actual composition. This is true even if one knows exactly what one wants to say, as I do. Often the process of writing clarifies and reveals possibilities of development and amplification that were not apparent in the outline. And, hopefully, the poetry itself, once it gets written, will have transformed the stiff, even pompous-sounding, formulas of the outline into the moving, living thing that we all want.

Appendix C

Letters Between John Finlay and Allen Tate (1966)

> UNIVERSITY OF ALABAMA
> UNIVERSITY, ALABAMA
>
> COLLEGE OF ARTS AND SCIENCES
> DEPARTMENT OF ENGLISH
>
> January 31, 1966
>
> Dear Mr. Tate,
>
> Forgive my boldness. A friend and I have just come from drinking beer. We started quoting your poems — as many as we could. We began to be like those travellers in "The Mediterranean" — briefly and tenuously in a world in which the spirit is at home. We praised your vision, your rage, your courage. Mr. Tate, I know this sounds silly but I am compelled to write you and thank you for your poems. They are so much a part of me, have helped me see so much of my own life that I can not imagine what I would be without them.
>
> May God bless you.
>
> Yours truly,
> John Finlay

John Finlay's Letter to Allen Tate
(Transcription on right hand page)

January 31, 1966

Dear Mr. Tate,

Forgive my boldness. A friend and I have just come from drinking beer. We started quoting your poems – as many as we could. We began to be like those travellers in "The Mediterranean" – briefly and tenuously in a world in which the spirit is at home. We praised your vision, your rage, your courage. Mr. Tate, I know this sounds silly but I am compelled to write you and thank you for your poems. They are so much a part of me, have helped me see so much of my own life that I can not imagine what I would be without them.

May God bless you,

Yours truly,
John Finlay

UNIVERSITY OF Minnesota

127 Vincent Hall COLLEGE OF LIBERAL ARTS
DEPARTMENT OF ENGLISH · MINNEAPOLIS, MINNESOTA 55455

February 18, 1966

Dear Mr. Finlay,

  In the course of a year I get a number of letters from strangers about my poems; but never in any year since I began to appear in print (that's a long time ago) have I received a letter that pleased me as much as yours does.

  What I usually get is some kind of "admiration", but this has been a little distant, or perhaps it would be more precise to say that the admiration is often qualified by some sort of question concerning what-does-it-mean? And of course I cannot tell them that. One's vanity, of course, is always with one; my own rating of myself, I confess, is not low; but I have never before been told that my poems have become a part of anybody's life. I am moved and grateful.

      Sincerely yours,

      Allen Tate

Mr. John Finlay

Allan Tate's letter to John Finlay
(Transcription on right hand page)

February 18, 1966

Dear Mr. Finlay,

In the course of a year I get a number of letters from strangers about my poems; but never in any year since I began to appear in print (that's a long time ago) have I received a letter that pleased me as much as yours does.

What I usually get is some kind of "admiration", but this has been a little distant, or perhaps it would be more precise to say that the admiration is often qualified by some sort of question concerning what-does-it-mean? And of course I cannot tell them that. One's vanity, of course, is always with one; my own rating of myself, I confess, is not low; but I have never before been told that my poems have become a part of anybody's life. I am moved and grateful.

Sincerely yours,

Allen Tate
[signature]

Mr. John Finlay

Appendix D

A Note on John Finlay and Allen Tate by David Middleton (2018)

Allen Tate (1899–1979) and Yvor Winters (1900–1968) were the two greatest influences on John Finlay as a writer both of poetry and of prose. Tate and Winters served as models for Finlay of the modern poet-critic, or man of letters, addressing the problems posed by modernity to our inherited Greco-Roman and Judeo-Christian culture. And, it should be noted, both Tate and Winters wrote traditional measured verse, as would Finlay after them.

For Winters, the answer to these modern problems was a combination of reason, stoicism, and "intellectual theism," a theism that Winters felt compelled to accept as the basis for a belief in absolutes. For Tate, the final answer was found in his conversion to Roman Catholicism. Of these two influences on Finlay, Tate was the earlier. Finlay kept Tate's letter of February 18, 1966 and hung it, framed, wherever he lived. (The original is now in the John Finlay Papers at Louisiana State University.)

Finlay first met Tate at the University of Alabama, Tuscaloosa, in the mid 1960s when Tate visited campus, probably for a poetry reading or lecture. A photograph has survived showing Finlay, Tate, and others at this event. The distinguished scholar of southern and American literature Lewis P. Simpson has commented on Tate's letter and this photograph: "Finlay's letter to Tate was written soon after Tate had come to the campus of the University of Alabama to fulfill a speaking engagement, and Finlay had met him in person for the first time. Tate's visit seems to have been sponsored by the Alabama graduate students in English, and Finlay was, one surmises, primarily responsible for the invitation to Tate. A photograph taken at the time shows him with Tate (the invariable cigarette dangling from the fingers of Tate's left hand), Tate's wife, Helen, and two other persons, presumably, like Finlay, graduate students. The predominant feature of the picture is the way in which Finlay has his eyes fixed on 'Master Tate.'"

"Master Tate" is taken from an epigram Finlay inscribed in his copy of Allen Tate's *Collected Essays* (1959):

John Martin Finlay [signature]

For Allen Tate

If now our lean language can sing
Of laurel and the rough dogwood
Caught in the single glow of faith
That brought the salty Aeneas to Rome,
It is because of MASTER TATE.

These lines clearly indicate that Tate showed Finlay how to be a modern yet traditional writer, employing "lean language" and being devoted to recovering and defending the classical-Christian past. Uniting the "laurel"—the Greco-Roman symbol of poetic achievement—and the "dogwood"—a tree whose cross-shaped blossoms with their petal-tips tinged rusty-red are associated with the Crucifixion, and also being a tree which is common in the American South—Finlay sees the journey of Virgil's Aeneas to Italy and the founding of Rome as at one with the Rome of Roman Catholicism, to which both Tate and Finlay converted: "Caught in the single glow of faith." And Finlay's reference to "the salty Aeneas" is almost certainly meant to call to mind Tate's poems "Aeneas at Washington" and "Aeneas at New York." There is also Finlay's own epigram "Aeneas in Modernity."

Moreover, in a page that has survived of his introduction of Tate at The University of Alabama, Finlay implicitly associates himself with Tate's major concern as a writer: "The voices in which Mr. Tate has spoken are indeed wonderfully many; yet there is a thematic unity in all he has written. As Mr. Andrew Lytle has said: Mr. Tate's theme is nothing more or less than what is left of Christendom. . . ."

Finlay met Tate on at least one other occasion—when Finlay was visiting southern agrarian writer Andrew Lytle. Finlay recorded this meeting in his diary: "August 25–28, 1966, I was the houseguest of Mr. Andrew Lytle at Monteagle, Tennessee. On August 27, 1966 Mr. Allen Tate who was staying at a nearby cottage (with his new bride) read two of my poems, the Sonnet + the moon piece, and said that they were "remarkable & excellent." *(I say this so that it will spur me on to more work, not to flatter my vanity.)* Mr. Lytle expressed similar views. Of course, I got some criticism too!"

Tate's influence appears not only in Finlay's poetry but also in his essays. In the "Introduction" to *Flaubert in Egypt and Other Essays*—his book on Gnosticism in modern literature and thought—Finlay uses Tate's late essay "Mere Literature and the Lost Traveller" (1979) as the basis of his own investigations of the sometimes subtle, even hidden presence of the Gnostic spirit in modernity. What Finlay says of Tate's essay on Gnosticism may be taken as a statement of the profound struggle Finlay endured in his personal life, analyzed in his literary works, and defeated at last by his conversion to Roman Catholicism and by the circumstances of his final, extended illness and early death, which Finlay said he accepted as purgatorial.

As Finlay states in the "Introduction," "I would imagine that Tate himself would have believed that Gnosticism is a recurrent temptation of fallen humanity and that the first Gnostic was Satan" and adds (perhaps thinking of his own case) that "the elusive gnostic spirit . . . frequently exists only in the indirections and implications of what the writer 'publically' says." This Gnosticism, Finlay continues, "is the idea of an ontological alienation of God from both the natural and human world. The desire to escape from this world, which Tate and the historians view as essential to all Gnosticisms, only results from the belief that God has abandoned the world to darkness, evil, and meaninglessness, and that there is no analogy between His pure essence and the gross matter of this world."

In his wide-ranging essay on Finlay's life and works, "The Romance of Modern Classicism: Remarks on the Life and Work of John Finlay, 1941–1991," Jeffrey Goodman concludes that "while Finlay's style inherits its mode of diction from Flaubert and the early Joyce and its sense of phrasing, in places, from Edgar Bowers (another Southerner), his poetic form is the heir to Tate refined by Winters."

But Tate was both the earlier and perhaps, in the end, the more profound influence on Finlay. As Lewis P. Simpson has argued, "there was a major difference between Winters and Tate, and the difference was all important to Finlay. Tate subscribed to a faith that transcends the 'intellectual theism' of Winters. The final sentence in [Tate's essay] 'The Man of Letters in the Modern World' is, 'The end of social man is a communion in time through love, which is above time.' In a step taken in the year in which he finished his dissertation on Winters, Finlay sealed what was already a long standing commitment to the way beyond by leaving the Episcopal communion and following Tate into the Roman Catholic faith."

Finlay also followed Tate in composing, late in his poetic career, shorter narrative poems with southern settings. Tate's "The Swimmers" and "The Buried Lake" (both first published in 1953) are matched by a number of Finlay's poems of the 1980s, including a group assembled and sequenced by Finlay himself as *The American Tragedies*, published as a chapbook only after Finlay's death.

One other connection between John Finlay and Allen Tate should be noted. In 1988, Harry Duncan, regarded by many as America's finest maker of hand-printed books, published on his renowned

Cummington Press John Finlay's chapbook *The Salt of Exposure*. This was the last collection Finlay would live to see into print.

Over the course of a lifetime, Duncan had published books of verse by some of America's greatest poets. These poets include William Carlos Williams, Wallace Stevens, Marianne Moore, and Robert Lowell—as well as Yvor Winters and Allen Tate.

In the correspondence between Finlay and Duncan concerning the publication of Finlay's chapbook, Finlay expressed his debt to Allen Tate. In reply, Duncan asked Finlay whether he knew that Allen Tate was Duncan's godfather and added, "How much he would have acclaimed your work!" Duncan's words take us back to Tate's 1966 letter to Finlay, who had written Tate to express his admiration for Tate's poetry. As Tate says at the end of his letter, "I have never before been told that my poems have become a part of anybody's life. I am moved and grateful."

To these exchanges may be added Finlay's comments in reply to Duncan in a letter of 12 June 1987: "It must be quite an honor to have had Allen Tate for your godfather. I admire the man immensely though I can't frequently get at the more obscure of his poems. I knew him slightly at Sewanee when he had come back South after his retirement. I now remember Lewis Simpson as having told me that he met you at one of Tate's birthday parties. He's buried at Sewanee and *Ave Maria* is written on his tomb. But you already knew this."[1]

In his Ph.D. dissertation, "'The Unfleshed Eye': A Study of Intellectual Theism in the Poetry and Criticism of Yvor Winters" (1980), Finlay linked his two literary fathers, Winters and Tate: "Allen Tate has described the main outline of Winters' poetry in the following terms: 'the poet stands perpetually at the edge of an abyss (or at the 'brink of darkness'), which he knows to be an abyss in spite of the fact that everybody else is eagerly trying to fall into it.'"

Like Winters, Finlay had looked over the brink of the abyss and then pulled back. Like Tate, he went further. As Finlay said in lines he chose from one of his own poems as the epigraph to the typescript of *Mind and Blood,* his collected poems left unpublished at his death, "In light apart from me, I seek the Word / Holding mind and blood from the absurd."

His seeking, and, at last, his finding of the Word became Finlay's lifelong journey that, like Tate's, ended in Rome, in death, and in that greater Rome beyond.

Appendix E

A Letter from John Finlay to Janet Lewis Winters on *The American Tragedies (1987)*

Aug. 5, 1987
Rt. 4, Bellwood Rd.
Enterprise, AL 36330

Dear Mrs. Winters,

I enjoyed reading your letter. The quote from your father's book interests me a great deal. I think what he says is the absolute truth. I am getting ready to write on the subject myself, and so I would like to read his book. It is the archaic Greek mind which particularly holds my attention. Why did the philosophical mind arise when and where it did—some such question I have been trying to get a hold on. The fact that the mind itself proves the existence of God has always struck me as true too. As long as you have an immaterial element in the mind—and memory proves such an element there—and believe that the mind did not create itself, then you have to posit as its cause an immaterial agent higher than the human being. Or so it seems to me and I am happy to learn your father too.

Would you do me a favor *if you have the time*? I've finished a group of poems most of which are based on stories my great-grandmother[1] told me as a child. She was a little girl during the Civil War and through her parents she knew of the Indian Wars before that. Do you think that the poems properly belong together or do you think they would be more profitably read separate from a sequence? They are all in blank verse and seem to adhere in my mind. But please don't fool with them unless you have the time. I ask you this favor because I value your criticism.

We are having a good summer. We got the rains when we had to have them, and the fig tree right now is getting ready to produce its second crop.

Sincerely,
John Finlay

P.S. I hope to visit California in the fall. If so, I would like to pay you an afternoon visit.[2]

Appendix F [1]

A Note on *The American Tragedies* by David Middleton (1997)

These six poems on American history, particularly southern history, were composed by Finlay in the mid-to-late 1980s. The stories on which he based most of the poems were told to him by his great-grandmother. This edition prints for the first-time versions that differ in some ways (including titles) from those scattered throughout *Mind and Blood: The Collected Poems of John Finlay* (1992). Finlay sent this six-poem collection in typescript to Janet Lewis, who sent it to me in 1991 shortly after Finlay's death. *The American Tragedies* stands as an achievement in and of itself, with each poem drawing out implications from the others when read together in sequence and in these versions.

As a whole, these poems make up a long meditation on such subjects as the sufferings of Native Americans on the Trail of Tears, anti-Catholic prejudice in the South (leading to a lynching of a Catholic immigrant), anti-Semitism, slavery, an early example of modern war in the poem "The Blood of Shiloh"—on the Civil War battle fought in Tennessee—and the brutality of frontier life in clashes between races, cultures, and religious prejudices. Finlay is unflinching in his descriptions of these matters, but there is also a loving sympathy for some of the people caught up in the American experiment, especially those drawn to the idea that America could somehow leave history behind and become a kind of second Eden.

A related poem not in the sequence, "The Exiles," dedicated to Janet Lewis, deals, like "The Pioneers," with the tragedy of the American Indians. Lewis' fine poems on the American Indians were an important influence not only on Finlay's poems on the subject, but also on the form and style of his several late, short narratives of life in the American South, including the six poems that make up the present collection. These poems, which Clive Wilmer has claimed exemplify a genre largely invented by Finlay, owe much else to Janet Lewis as well, especially in those passages containing a gentle restraint, a quietly understated tone, a luminous simplicity of line, and a deeply sympathetic concern and loving regard for others caught up in personal or historical tragedy.

Appendix G

Mind and Blood: John Finlay (1941–1991)
by David Middleton (1991)[1]

When John Finlay died on the morning of February 17, 1991, for me a literary friendship of nearly twenty years came to an end. I first met John in 1971 at the wedding of a friend and found him then, as ever, a person who had long ago totally committed himself to the life of the mind and to the expression of that life in letters.

John Finlay was born on January 24, 1941, in Ozark, Alabama, and grew up on his family's farm outside Enterprise. His mother recalls that as a boy John would read Shakespeare's plays in between loading fertilizer into the hoppers and would recite lines from Shakespeare to the cows (whom he named for Greek goddesses) as he took them to and from the pasture every day. These stories and others, such as a childhood friend's memory of John always reading on the bus ride to and from school and a high-school teacher's recollection of John's outburst in a class that had been studying Longfellow—"This is such inferior writing!"—indicate that John was destined to be a man of letters from a very early period in his life.

After earning his B.A. (1964) and M.A. (1966) at the University of Alabama at Tuscaloosa, a school he entered by performing the remarkable feat of making the highest possible score in English and the lowest possible score in math, John taught for four years at the University of Montevallo (formerly Alabama College). Thereafter, except for a year in Europe (especially in Paris), and including a memorable six months on the Greek island of Corfu, John spent most of the rest of the 1970s as a doctoral student in English at Louisiana State University.

During his years in Baton Rouge, John grew into full maturity as a poet, completed his dissertation on Yvor Winters' intellectual theism, and began work on the essays that would make up *Flaubert in Egypt and Other Essays,* his profound study of the modern world's apostasy from the permanent clarities of the Aristotelian-Thomistic synthesis. (John converted to Roman Catholicism in 1980.) In carrying forward this dual career as poet and essayist, John was following not only Yvor Winters but also Allen Tate, an unpublished early poem to whom survives as well as a photograph of John and Tate at a literary gathering in the 1960s and a framed letter from Tate thanking John for a letter on Tate's poetry. Tate wrote: "I have never before been told that my poems have become a part of anybody's life. I am moved and grateful."

Those of us who knew John at LSU in the 1970s recall him as a wonderful conversationalist. With a Scotch held firmly in one hand and gesticulating fervently with a cigarette in the other, John would occasionally rivet us all with episodes from the latest chapter of his literary life, a life he lived with all the passion and drama of a love affair. Otherwise, he often remained quietly serious in company, sometimes even reading by himself, and though possessed of a short temper, he held himself to the rituals of courtesy in the old southern style. Both in his speech and in his writing, John had a way of piercing deeply in simple, precise language toward what, in a late poem, he called "plainest naked truth." He was certainly witty—describing Robert Bridges (whose best poems he loved) as "a Shelley who played football at Oxford instead of writing *The Necessity of Atheism*" and once commenting at 4:00 A.M. when, after a late party, antacids were being passed around, "Ah, the modern sacrament!"

After I left Baton Rouge in 1977 for Nicholls State University in Thibodaux and John returned permanently to the farm in Alabama in 1981, I came to know him better than I had done at LSU. For many years, we exchanged essays and poems and wrote letters critiquing each other's work. A dramatic late-night phone call from John when he had just finished a new poem was always thrilling. Eventually we shared the pleasure of seeing each other's initial poetry chapbooks in print thanks to R. L. Barth, our first publisher.

During these years John was intensely reading the Greeks. As he said to me in a letter of October 6, 1982: "The Greeks satisfy me in the deepest possible way. We should never, never get very far away from them. Let's learn Greek in our old age and meet death in a clean room with only a few well-worn Greek texts in our hands." John loved not only Greek thought but also the beauty of the Greek isles to which he always wanted to return. As he wrote in 1984, "I shall never forget the experience of sunlight when I lived on Corfu—the clarity, the brilliance of objects defined in unambiguous light. I could cry thinking about it."

When I heard that John was ill with AIDS, I called him at once and stayed in touch by letter and by phone every week until the end. At times, John felt depressed about his work becoming known, yet in the end he returned to a view expressed to me in 1982: "We must bear our isolation.... what are we to do but work and pray?" John did live to see the first reviews of his poetry begin to appear, and he was able to enjoy *A Garland for John Finlay*, which was printed in November of 1990. This small book contained one poem each by many of the British and American poets whose work John most admired. In fact, just as he was taken ill, John had begun to move within a wider circle of poets outside the South. This recognition led, in 1987, to a trip to the University of California at Santa Barbara, where, through the good offices of Edgar Bowers and Dick Davis, John gave a rare public reading of his poems.

In the final telephone conversation we were able to hold, in December 1990, John, having entrusted me with finding a publisher for his collected poems, slowly spoke the title he had chosen for such a collection—*Mind and Blood*. This title seems to me to sum up John Finlay's literary life. Both in his essays and in his poems, John sought to defend and celebrate the human mind as that agency by which alone the created world can be known as divinely ordained, objectively real, and essentially good. With Aquinas, he believed that knowledge begins for us with the sensuous particulars of nature (blood); but John also insisted on the equally real transcendent universals of abstract thought (mind). John was vividly aware of the existence of God and accepted as true the ancient orders of the angels and of the beings of creation. And he was convinced of the reality of Satan as a maimed, malignant being of high, perverse intelligence and subtlest guile, the modern disbelief in whom terrified him as Satan's great victory over man since the fall from the Garden itself.

I have never known anyone for whom the drama of the life of the mind was so traumatically real and so crucially important as it was for John Finlay. That importance, along with the greatness of soul that so many of us think of as John's essential character, is captured in "A Prayer to the Father," deliberately written as his final poem in the spring of 1990. There, in twelve plain lines, the dying poet gives back at last God's most precious gift to him, his human intellect:

A Prayer to the Father

Death is not far from me. At times I crave
The peace I think that it will bring. Be brave,
I tell myself, for soon your pain will cease.
But terror still obtains when our long lease
On life ends at last. Body and soul,
Which fused together should make up one whole
Suffer deprived as they are wrenched apart.
O God of love and power, hold still my heart
When death, that ancient, awful fact appears;
Preserve my mind from all deranging fears,
And let me offer up my reason free
And where I thought, there see Thee perfectly.

Appendix H

John Finlay and the Situation of the Southern Writer
by Lewis P. Simpson (1999)[1]

Figure to yourself a man stopping at the gate of a Confederate graveyard on a late autumn afternoon
—Allen Tate, "Narcissus as Narcissus" (1938)

Like all Southerners who began to aspire to a literary career after his fame became universal and his presence overwhelming, the young John Martin Finlay held Faulkner in awe. Learning of his death in the summer of 1962, Finlay, who had just completed his sophomore year at the University of Alabama, commemorated the event in a poem. As preserved in his papers it reads:

> He died in the midst of a hot summer—
> The land cracked and dried, waiting for rain
> And the heat waves dancing drunkenedly [*sic*]
> Over the earth that still carried its curse
> Like a packet of old, dirty letters
> Containing the ageless threats.
> His home, his land for a moment
> Paid tribute on the radios and television
> Interspersed with notices of bomb-explosions
> Ripping up the bowels of the earth,
> And promised tax reductions.
> The artist in his death finding
> Room among the meaningless rabble.
> When we heard it, we felt a panic—
> Suddenly, realizing how few we are,
> With the senseless night full of
> Idiotic laughter forced from sick lungs,
> Stealing upon us, engulfing us.
> We need our artists. Among the
> Yelping and howling of hungry wolfs [*sic*]
> They weave the magic web of thought
> And remind us of things likely forgotten
> In times of hunger and evils—
> The old verities of the human heart.[2]

Perhaps the most notable feature of this early, rather clumsy poetic effort, with its echo of Faulknerian rhetoric, is its ambivalent focus on the "editorial we." In the context of the whole poem the "we" in the line, "Suddenly realizing how few we are," intimates that it may be read as "Suddenly realizing how few we artists are." As the young Faulkner would have boldly assumed had he been memorializing a famous poet, the youthful Finlay assumed, though hesitantly, that he was paying a tribute to a fellow literary artist.

The development of Finlay's commitment to the literary vocation may be traced to some extent through family recollections of his life while he was growing up on his father's peanut farm, which was located close to the small south Alabama town named Enterprise. Not far from Enterprise was the older community of Ozark, the home of John Finlay's grandmother, where John was born on January 24, 1941. After the family moved to the Enterprise farm, John frequently spent weekends in his grandmother's house in Ozark. Although one can only conjecture that he inherited his inclination to literature from his now deceased great-grandfather, he would seem to have found a prime source of literary inspiration in his deceased great-grandfather's library of classic authors. Another source of inspiration John found in Ozark was the friendship he formed with one of his grandmother's friends, Annie Laurie Cullens, who, according to John's mother, Jean Sorrell Finlay, "shared a love of literature" with John and "had a strong influence on his life." By the time he was old enough to help on the farm, his mother recalls, he had become such an avid reader that he found ways to combine chores and books. In particular, Jean Finlay remembers how John read Shakespeare during the intervals that occurred in his task of loading fertilizer hoppers. She also recalls how he circumvented the order of his stern father that all of the family must be in bed by eight o'clock at night by pretending to be asleep, and then, when he knew his father was asleep, turning a light on and reading until midnight; how, while he was bringing the family cow from the pasture, he could be heard reciting Shakespearean passages to her; how, according to report, he kept his nose in a book while on the bus ride to and from school. Through his constant reading John not only acquired a far better literary education than his peers but tended to develop passionate convictions about writers he liked and disliked. One of his high school teachers remembers having to reprove him for a patronizing critique of his fellow students for liking Longfellow, who was, he explained, far inferior to Keats and Shelley—an opinion he was to repudiate later on when he became a severe critic of all the romantics.[3]

But not all of John's reading during his high school years was in the standard textbook authors. When he was about fifteen, he became fascinated with Margaret Mitchell's *Gone with the Wind*. In a well-worn 1954 edition of the novel he scribbled:

> Scarlett represents the South and Rhett what the South had lost in the bellum [*sic*]. [S]he could not think of getting him back in such a time as it is but "tomorrow is another day." In my thin[k]ing we are still thin[k]ing and tomorrow is another day. You cannot kill what is in a true So[u]therner. Do you suppose this time and day would kill the spirit of Scallett [*sic*]. I hope not. But it has killed the spirit of many Southerners. I am not dead yet.[4]

According to his teacher in his senior year in high school, Jean Finlay says, John went through a period when he "loved" Thomas Wolfe, although as far as I have determined he left no record of his passion for Wolfe.[5] At this time, though again a specific record of his initial acquaintance with them does not seem to co-exist, he was very likely discovering other well-known "Vanderbilt Agrarians": Tate, Robert Penn Warren, John Crowe Ransom, Donald Davidson, and Andrew Lytle.

In any event, at whatever time he first read Wolfe, Faulkner, Tate *et al*, the young Finlay did so in the context of an intangible dimension of his early literary education: his association with a great-grandmother, who was old enough to have childhood recollections of the Civil War. In 1987 when he sent me a copy of his poem "The Blood of Shiloh," he said:

> The poem is based on what my great-grandmother told me about her father. I hope I've got all the history right. I knew her in her extreme old age when she didn't have quite total control over her facts. She said once, for instance, that as a child she put her head to the iron railing on the rail-road, and heard the cannon of the Battle of Mobile just then taking place.[6]

Through stories her parents had told her, Finlay's great-grandmother also knew about the Indian wars before the time of the Civil War.[7] Indeed, she provided what was already becoming a comparatively rare resource of the southern literary imagination by the time Finlay was born, the experience of being in contact, either through living remembrance, or the remembrance of remembrance, with the time of the Civil War and its context in the time both before and after the South's defeat. Although the weakening of the chain of southern memory is evident in Finlay, in his remembrance of the fragile voice of his great-grandmother the past that was still present to him, and the subtle process of the memory at work on his imagination eventually became the source of some of his most striking poems.

But before this happened, before it could happen, John Finlay's sense of the literary vocation required a model for its development less overpowering, less inhibiting than that of the South's Nobel laureate, under whose "shadow," he wrote in one journal entry, we are "like ants nibbling the feet of a giant."[8] He was to discover a more congenial model in Allen Tate. Although Tate wrote more critical essays than poems, if we are to judge by an inscription in Finlay's copy of Tate's *Collected Essays* (1959), his primary attraction was to the poet:

> If now our lean language can sing
> Of laurel and the rough dogwood
> Caught in the single glow of faith
> That brought the salty Aeneas to Rome,
> It is because of MASTER TATE.[9]

Finlay apparently wrote this at the time he acquired his copy of the *Collected Essays*–between 1959 and the early 1960s. By this point the poet who had imagined "Aeneas at Washington" and "Aeneas at New York" had obviously become a decisive influence on him. In 1966, when he was working on his M.A. degree at the University of Alabama, Finlay had written a letter to Tate expressing his personal gratitude for his poetry and saying that Tate's poems had become a part of his life. Tate replied that he in turn was grateful to Finlay, declaring that he had never been told that his poems had "become a part of anybody's life." Finlay treasured Tate's response. David Middleton has told me that Finlay framed it and kept it on his wall everywhere he lived. "Tate somehow showed Finlay the way," Middleton observes.[10]

Finlay's letter to Tate was written soon after Tate had come to the campus of the University of Alabama to fulfill a speaking engagement, and Finlay had met him in person for the first time. Tate's visit seems to have been sponsored by the Alabama graduate students in English, and Finlay was, one surmises, primarily responsible for the invitation to Tate. A photograph taken at the time shows him with Tate (the invariable cigarette dangling from the fingers of Tate's left hand), Tate's wife, Helen, and two other persons, presumably, like Finlay, graduate students. The predominant feature of the picture is the way in which Finlay has his eyes fixed on "Master Tate."[11]

But a more significant relic of Tate's appearance in Tuscaloosa is what Finlay said when he introduced him. Although only the first page of the introductory comment is to be found in his papers, the fragment affords a summation of an influence on Finlay that by this point had clearly become decisive. It shows, moreover, that, if he ignored this in the inscription he placed in his copy of the collected essays, the whole body of Tate's work had become a shaping influence on the young Finlay. Introducing Tate, he said:

> We must acknowledge a debt as best we can. If the poets and critics help us to see our world and to "know the time" (to borrow from one of Mr. Tate's poems), when I am sure many of us here tonight have a special debt to pay Allen Tate. I am thinking of all those whose reading of a short story by Henry James or a poem by John Donne has become more exact and perceptive because of a knowledge of Mr. Tate's criticism, as well as of the apprentice poets who have learned to use their language more effectively after carefully studying the techniques of his own verse. Of course, we can never fully pay this kind of debt. But we can humbly and gratefully acknowledge it, which we now do.

Finlay went on to indicate a greater, more crucial debt we owe to Tate, this for the nature of the vision he has projected in his work: "The voices in which Mr. Tate has spoken to us are indeed wonderfully many: yet there is a thematic unity in all he has written. As Mr. Andrew Lytle has said, 'Mr. Tate's theme is nothing more or less than what is left of Christendom.'" In a sentence that breaks off at the end of the surviving page of the introduction but may easily be completed, Finlay added: "And I think Mr. Lytle meant not merely the purely Christian vision, but also the whole heritage of [the classical-Christian tradition]."[12]

By the time he wrote his introduction of Tate, Finlay implies that he had, through Tate and Lytle and others of the now fabled Agrarian group, become aware both of the central motive of modern literature and the relation of the writer of the twentieth-century American South to it.

The motive is to be found in a manifold effort to explore and depict the often highly ironic implications of the vision of the modern world as existing in a civilizational crisis that, since it is the result of the progressive loss of its essential heritage, the Hebraic-Christian-classical tradition, can be resolved by nothing less than a recovery of this heritage by the poet (in the root sense of the term, not only the versifier but the novelist, dramatist, essayist, or anyone who possesses a "creative imagination"). The relation of southern writers to this motive is to be found in their struggle to incorporate the vision of the modern literary situation in their poems, stories, plays, and essays. In their struggle to interpret the history of the American South as a version, essentially mythic, of the modern world as a whole, that is to say, we find the motive of Faulkner, Tate, Lytle, Donald Davidson, Caroline Gordon, Katherine Anne Porter, Eudora Welty, Robert Penn Warren, and all the others who may be referred to as belonging to the period of the twenties, thirties, and forties, or the time commonly known as the "Southern Renascence."

After writing about it for thirty years or more, Tate offered a summary explanation of the pursuit of this motive in an essay he called "A Southern Mode of the Literary Imagination" (1959). Essentially, Tate describes how the more perceptive members of the generation of post-World War I southern writers altered their situation by replacing an inherited mode of rhetorical discourse with the modern mode of dialectical discourse:

> The Southern legend, as Malcolm Cowley has called it, of defeat and heroic frustration was taken over by a dozen or more first-rate writers and converted into a universal myth of the human condition. W.B. Yeats's great epigram points to the nature of the shift from melodramatic rhetoric to the dialectic of tragedy: "Out of the quarrel with others we make rhetoric; out of the quarrel with ourselves, poetry."[13]

Yeats' epigram is strikingly applicable to "Ode to the Confederate Dead" and to "Narcissus as Narcissus," the essay Tate wrote in the years after the publication about his most famous poem. Pointing out that "Ode to the Confederate Dead" is "about" solipsism . . . or about Narcissism, or any other *ism* that denotes the failure of the human personality to function objectively in nature and society," the author of the "Ode" implies a sense of identity with the plight of the figure at the gate. Like his protagonist, who is close to being but is not quite his persona, he recognizes that in "the fragmentary cosmos" of the modern scientific-industrial society, he has expended "his energy piecemeal over separate functions that ought to come under a unity of being." Like the man at the gate he also recognizes that in his acute awareness of this situation he has imprisoned himself in "the remarkable self-consciousness of our age"; and, being in this state of spiritual paralysis, lacks the capacity to seek salvation from his dilemma. Yet in the very act of meditating on his situation, the man at the gate also realizes that he has not altogether yielded to it. He is still capable of experiencing the nostalgic possibility of recovering a society that had once been moved by the "active faith" symbolized by the heroic virtue the Confederate dead exemplify.[14]

But, although he identifies himself with the deeply introverted man at the gate, the poet, the creator of the man at the gate, distinguishes between himself as Narcissus and his shadowy protagonist as Narcissus. His dilemma is not quite so exclusive. In the poetic act of conceiving this figure the author has objectified his feeling of identity with him by in effect answering the challenge the protagonist issues in his question, "What shall we say who have knowledge / Carried to the heart?" He has written a poem in which he represents the conflict in the modern intellect between the scientific view of man and nature and the ancient desires of the heart in such concentrated form that the form becomes "visible," not "as a logical dilemma," but in "Mr. R.P. Blackmur's phrase, as 'experienced form.'"[15] In contrast to the experience the poet customarily represents in an ode, that of bearing witness to the experience of seeing the public drama of celebrating an heroic act, the poet of "Ode to the Confederate Dead" has ironically represented the experience of bearing witness to the private dramas of a lone man meditating at a graveyard gate. In a basic sense of course Tate's poem is about a public quarrel inspired by a question that has become more and more insistent since in the invention of the telescope Galileo internalized the world and the universe in the mind of man: Is the destiny of human experience properly expressed in the scientific or the religious view of man? In a complex sense, it is about an experience that has been going on for almost the same span of time, namely, the internalization of this quarrel in the mind of the poet. In a still more specific, and yet complex, sense "Ode to the Confederate Dead" is a representation of the subtle dialectical drama—the subjective "dialect of tragedy"—experienced in the mind of a poet who was a highly self-conscious member of the third generation of writers in the American South since its defeat in the war of 1861–1865—the generation whose careers began in the years between the two great wars of the twentieth century.

The historical context of this drama—the formative years of the author of "Ode to the Confederate Dead" (Tate was born in 1899)—is far removed from the historical context of the formative period of Finlay's writing. Born in the year of Pearl Harbor, Finlay began the career his childhood interests had anticipated in the years of the Vietnam debacle, when he was a student at the University of Alabama (B.A. and M.A. in English, 1964, 1966). While at Alabama he wrote poems for *Comment,* the campus literary magazine, and in his senior year served as its editor. The publication of an interview Finlay did with Eudora Welty was an especially notable feature of *Comment* during this year. At the same time, while serving as research assistant to Hudson Strode, who was working on his biography and edition of the letters of Jefferson Davis, Finlay found himself digging into the history of the rise and fall of the Confederacy. A more crucial stage of Finlay's career began, when, after teaching at a small Alabama college for four years, he entered the graduate program in English at Louisiana State University, where he remained, save for two years in Europe (1972–73), until he was awarded the Ph.D. degree in English literature in 1980.

Before coming to LSU—at least as far back as 1965, his notebooks indicate—Finlay had discovered a second literary model in the poet-critic Yvor Winters (1900–1968), who, in David Middleton's words, was "the most prominent American defender and master practitioner of traditional measured verse during the height of the free-verse rebellion."[16] In fact, in what is the most authoritative and challenging essay on Finlay yet written, Middleton says that Finlay entered into the graduate program in English at LSU after reading an essay on "Classicism and the Modern Poet" (*Southern Review,* 1969) by one of the leading proponents of Winters, the poet-critic Donald E. Stanford, who was a member of the graduate faculty in English at LSU. As Middleton also points out, however, Finlay's interest in Winters was not simply in his advocacy of formalism in poetry; it was in both the poetic and the philosophical principles that Winters "vividly embodied in his poetry and articulated [his] prose."[17] Eventually, under the direction of Stanford, Finlay wrote a distinguished doctoral dissertation entitled "The Unfleshed Eye: A Study of Intellectual Theism in the Poetry and Criticism of Yvor Winters."

In general, Finlay's interest in Winters was compatible with his devotion to Tate. Although Winters was not a Southerner, and differed widely from Tate in some respects, especially in his views about God, Winters and Tate were alike in their adherence to (1) the view that poetic composition is a formal discipline and (2) their conception of the duty of the poet-critic as a social being to offer a rational, admonitory analysis of the moral and spiritual dilemmas of the modern world—or as Tate says in concluding his essay on "The Man of Letters in the Modern World," "to supervise the culture of language, to which the rest of culture is subordinate, and to warn us when our language is ceasing to forward the ends proper to man."[18]

But there was a major difference between Winters and Tate, and the difference was all important to Finlay. Tate subscribed to a faith that transcends the "intellectual theism" of Winters. The final sentence in "The Man of Letters in the Modern World" is, "The end of social man is a communion in time through love, which is above time."[19] In a step taken in the year in which he finished his dissertation on Winters, Finlay sealed what was already a long standing commitment to the way beyond by leaving the Episcopal communion and following Tate into the Roman Catholic faith.

In the same year (1980) Finlay became a convert to Catholicism, he decided that in the next phase of his literary career he would follow Tate by, ironically, actually doing what Tate and some of his fellows in the Agrarian movement of the 1930s had thought of doing, but, save for Andrew Lytle, never actually did: leave the academy to join the intellectual life and the life of the farmer. As he must have known, this had not worked for Lytle, but, in spite of the difficulties he and his family faced in a time when agriculture in America was being transformed into agribusiness, the return to the Enterprise farm—which at some time after his childhood years had been transformed from a peanut farm into a peanut and dairy farm—worked for Finlay. What turned out sadly to be the last decade of his life also proved to be the most productive.

In letters and notes—and in frequent conversations with me on the telephone (he fell into the pattern of phoning me every month or two, not for chit-chat but to have an extended discussion about some literary or philosophical topic)—Finlay mingled mentions of life on the farm with accounts of his reading, thought, and writing, showing, I think, that he experienced a sustaining sense of connection between his devotion to poetry and philosophy and his life on the farm. This sense of connection had more to do with the realities of life on the farm than with its pastoral pleasures. There were such pleasures: naming his favorite animals in the dairy herd for Greek gods and goddesses; listening to "the summer [droning] on in the great heated hum of things"; being awakened in the early morning by "the strangest sound coming from the woods in front of the house" and "thinking at first [that] it was a dying man screaming for help," then realizing that it was "hound dogs treeing a coon."[20] But Finlay had not gone back to Enterprise lured by the image of a pastoral retreat. He knew the realities of farm life, and it was these that sustained him when he returned to this life. One of the most arresting moments in his letters to me is a response to my recollection that when I was a kid and had the duty of milking two or three cows every day, I conceived the notion that it would be a great boon if a cow could be bred that required milking only once a week. "Yes, it would be a boon if they could invent a cow that gave milk once a week," he wrote. "Do you remember washing all the dirt and shit from those swollen bags? Well, that's what I have to do this afternoon. But I can't help but like the cows—they are good Thomistic animals and save one from the madness of Berkeley."[21]

The sanity of Aquinas vs. *the madness of Berkeley.* This opposition symbolizes a spiritual and intellectual anxiety that Finlay's confirmation in the Catholic faith had not resolved, but afterwards, in spite of his extensive reading in Aquinas and in modern Catholic apologists like Jacques Maritain, had become even more urgent. Finlay returned to the farm, one may be justified in saying, so that he could intensify his effort to resolve the quarrel with himself that had animated his dissertation on Winters. Although by the time he wrote this study, literary and religious motives had become inextricably blended in his thought and emotion, Finlay had recognized this quarrel fifteen years earlier in his introduction of Tate at Alabama. Cogently suggested in "Ode to the Confederate Dead," it is explicitly characterized in "Religion and the Old South," the essay Tate contributed to the Agrarian manifesto *I'll Take My Stand* (1930):

> They [the old southerners] had a religious life, but it was not organized with a right mythology. In fact, their rational life was not powerfully united to the religious experience, as it was in medieval society, and they are a fine specimen of the tragic pitfall upon which the Western mind has always hovered. . . . Since there is, in the Western mind, a radical division between the religious, the contemplative, the qualitative, on the one hand, and the scientific, the natural, the practical, on the other, the scientific mind always plays havoc with the spiritual life when it is not powerfully enlisted in its cause; it cannot be permitted to operate alone.[22]

What will prevent the scientific mind from operating alone? The Southerner must realize, Tate said, that "had she possessed a sufficient faith in her own kind of God," and thus been "able to bring out a body of doctrine setting forth her true conviction that the ends of man require more for their realization than politics," the South would not have been defeated in the War for Southern Independence. If she is now able to formulate such a doctrine "the setback of the war" will prove to have been "a very trivial one." But even if the South should realize its "true conviction," how can she express it? The answer, Tate says, is by violence. Paradoxically, the Southerner "must use an instrument, which is political, and so unrealistic and pretentious, that he cannot believe in it, to re-establish a private, self-contained, and essentially spiritual life."[23]

The paradox of Tate's challenge to the Southerner (precisely speaking, the southern writer, the southern intellectual) to take objective action—heroic, revolutionary action—in order to "reestablish a private self-contained, essentially spiritual life" is, as Tate acknowledges, "unrealistic and pretentious"; and, as he almost but not quite acknowledges, no more than a rhetorical metaphor. In offering his challenge Tate denied the reality of the historical South in favor of a mythic history that would serve as a metaphor for the sense of impending disaster in Western civilization envisioned generally by post-World War I European and American writers. Linking the South's failure to attain its independence to its failure to create a religion compatible with what Tate referred to with awesome simplicity as "the tradition"—by which he meant the tradition of referring the meaning of history to the faith in the concept of eternal truth as established in the late Middle Ages by the classical-Christian, or Aristotelian-Thomistic, synthesis—Tate suggested that the history of the South is a metaphor for world disaster.

But this epic sense of the meaning of southern history did not survive in the southern imagination beyond the Second World War, when the possibility of such an interpretation was displaced by an essentially subjective, "existentialist" vision of the fate of modern man. In the 1940s we find Robert Penn Warren writing novels that in a way may be said to reflect the dialectical mode Tate associated with an encompassing vision of the South as a microcosm of the modern world, but may be said to more nearly reflect the existential struggle of the lonely individual to find a way to take responsibility for his actions in a world divested of a sense of divine authority. In the 1950s and '60s, we find writers emerging—Flannery O'Connor, Walker Percy, Shelby Foote, William Styron, Elizabeth Spencer, Reynolds Price, Madison Jones, Walter Sullivan, and Ellen Douglas—who, even though, in varying ways, they may be regarded as struggling to redefine the vision of their predecessors, primarily offer testimony to the fading power of the image in the southern literary imagination of the South as an emblem of the classical-Christian heritage. When we come to the writers of Finlay's generation, those who emerged in the later sixties, the seventies, and the eighties, we discover that the vision that produced the Renascence—the vision of the South as what is left of Christendom—has ceased to be a motive in the southern literary imagination.

John Finlay's career is at once an exception and a tragic representation of this situation in later twentieth-century southern letters. In saying this I am thinking primarily of the tension in Finlay's poems and essays created, on the one hand, by his desire to achieve the lofty, authoritarian perspective, seemingly detached and impersonal, he saw exemplified in the poetry and criticism of Eliot and Tate, and, on the other hand, by his feeling that the literary expression of truth depends—as in varying ways it does in, say, O'Connor, Percy, and Styron—on the recognition of the individual's existential experience in living life. Finlay was aware of this tension early on, as we see in a reproachful warning he gave to himself in a journal entry in the 1960s:

> On looking back over these notes, I am struck with the connection between a person's private life and his public art—I have been so thoroughly in agreement with Eliot, et al. And their detachment, etc., until now . . . [sic] You must live more, whatever that overused verb means . . . [sic] and I know your art will improve, Mr. Finlay, you lazy no-count.[24]

And Finlay did live more, and his art did improve. But at a terrible price. We can estimate the price by reading the record of private life in his journals, diaries, and letters, but we can reckon it more surely by reading the implied record of his private life in the essays and poems that constitute his "public art."

Commenting on the essays, David Middleton observes that "Finlay, of course, was too shrewd not to know that [the] two processes of objective analysis and subjective psychoanalysis were simultaneously present" in them. Middleton refers to a letter Finlay wrote to him about his essays in December 1981 in which he posed the rhetorical question: "Have you thought of how our criticism so seemingly 'objective' and disinterested turns out almost against our will to be a sort of spiritual autobiography in disguise?"[25] "Almost against our will" is a way of saying "with our will"—or with my will. I remember Finlay once asked me if he should do away with the "I" in his essays. I said no; sensing that if he did this in the presumed interest of increasing the impression of his objectivity, he would be falsifying his true impulse in writing them, but not quite realizing at that time that Finlay really was asking not of me but of himself, whether or not he should try to obscure the way in which the essays represent his own deeply troubled spiritual situation.

This was the situation of a self-conscious descendant of Allen Tate, an eminent example, to paraphrase Walker Percy, of an "old modern" southern writer, trying to make his way in a "post-modern world."[26] It was the situation of a southern writer in the late twentieth century trying to define his dilemma in terms of a heritage that itself had become virtually undefinable. Finlay's attempt to cope with this problem is recorded in three collections of poems: *The Wide Porch and Other Poems*, 1984; *Between the Gulfs*, 1986; *The Salt of Exposure*, 1988, and the uncollected poems he published in the eighties; and in *Hermetic Light: Essays on the Gnostic Spirit in Modern Literature and Thought*, 1994, a book composed of essays he wrote in the eighties.

Hermetic Light–which, as Middleton observes in his "Afterword" to this book, takes its "text" from "Mere Literature and the Lost Traveller," the last essay Tate wrote—is, according to what Finlay once told me, about "the gods of modern literature, the various kinds of divinity, etc."[27] Another way to put this would be to say that like Tate in more than one essay it is about the alienation of God from mind in a post-Christian world. In addition, the more one reads these essays, the more one realizes that, if we consider what the term "poetry" means in the generic sense, Finlay's essays may be read in much the same way as the more varied essays of Tate may be read as being a part of the poetry he wrote, the essays and the poetry altogether constituting the text of an autobiographical poem about a poet's search for salvation. The experience of writing this autobiography might be characterized in the words Finlay used to describe what the writing of the essays in *Hermetic Light* had been like: "I feel as if the whole thing were a journey through hell or rather that *cloaca* St. Peter talks about in Dante."[28]

But Finlay's sense of his role in the drama he portrays in his writings is far more subdued than that which sustained Tate, who in "The Profession of the Writer in the South," could imagine the southern writer in a world historical situation comparable to that of Shakespeare in the age of the first Elizabeth. Comparatively speaking, whereas Tate's essays and poems reflect the sense of a southern poet who was personally at once involved in an epochal historical drama and a detached observer of it, Finlay's reflect the sense of an actor participating in an obscure drama he cannot with any assurance even name. Finlay's poems and essays, in other words, dramatize his role in an uncertain search for salvation in a terrifying century during which human beings have at once measurably expanded the average life span and overpopulated the world, while killing more of their own kind than in any prior age.

Middleton compares Finlay's essays in *Hermetic Light* to Hopkins' "sonnets of desolation": "Just as Hopkins tried to do" in those sonnets, "so . . . Finlay strives to locate, define, and resolve a dark conflict at the core of his being and thus to emerge into the light."[29] Possibly there is an echo of Hopkins in a letter in which he commented that the theme of a new collection of stories by an Alabama friend is "the desolation of the New South."[30] Unlike Tate, who wrote a number of essays, as well as poems and fiction on the desolation of the South, Finlay wrote neither essays nor stories on this theme but he did write a number of poems on it, among them some of his best. In these Finlay's awareness of "the dark conflict at the core of his being," if not more evident, is more poignantly present than in his essays. It may be too, that, in spite of the theme of the capacity of human beings to survive the evil in them, the promise of the emergence into the light is but faintly perceived. I am thinking in particular about a small collection Finlay sent me in manuscript copy in 1986 bearing the title "The American Tragedies: A Chronology of Six Poems." I am not quite sure why he chose this title, since the poems—all of them "pretty bleak" he remarked to me in conversation—are about life in the South from the time of the dispossession of the native inhabitants to the poet's own time. I suppose he meant to suggest that the tragic history of the South cannot be separated from the history of the nation, and that the poems in truth are about the desolation of America.

I don't know that John Finlay ever stopped at the gate of a Confederate graveyard on an autumn afternoon, or on any afternoon. Even if we knew that at some time he did do so, we could not, so far as I am aware, locate in published or unpublished sources an indication that Finlay in any explicit sense identified himself with the lonely figure in Allen Tate's famous poem. Yet the student of his life and thought and emotion, perceiving the dramatic relation between Finlay and "the mediating" southerner whose introspective reflections are recorded in "Ode to the Confederate Dead," must believe that on some late autumn afternoon—when the living memory of the Confederacy had passed into twilight and the twilight was verging on darkness—he did stop at the gate of a place where Confederate dead lie buried. I would suggest furthermore that, ironically, we well may imagine we see in Finlay a more intense, and a more conclusive, indeed a final embodiment of the intellectual and emotional situation of the twentieth-century southern poet Tate depicts in the figure at the gate than we see in Tate himself or in any of his contemporaries.

Andrew Lytle must have sensed this when Finlay was his guest at the Log Cabin in Monteagle, Tennessee, on March 11–12, 1967. David Middleton calls attention to one of the most evocative entries in his sporadic diary where Finlay says of this visit: "Later Mr. L[ytle] looked over at me and said that my face was old-fashioned, it was the first time he had noticed it and that I should have died in the 1863."³¹ But Finlay had not, and he knew it; and that made all the difference.

Appendix I

The Poetry of John Finlay by Donald E. Stanford (1991)[1]

[*The Southern Review*, Summer, 1991]

"Now held forever in the lean, hard line"
—"Audubon at Oakley," Finlay

I first met John Finlay in December 1969 when he drove from Alabama to Baton Rouge for an interview. He wished to study for the doctorate at Louisiana State University, beginning in 1970. He had become interested in the poetry and criticism of Yvor Winters; he had read my recent remarks in *The Southern Review* on Winters as a classical poet, and he wanted me to direct his dissertation on Winters. Shortly thereafter he entered LSU. It took him ten years to complete his dissertation, but it turned out to be one of the best I have ever directed. Its subject, intellectual theism in the work of Winters, was seminal for a series of essays which he wrote on various writers during the 1980s. The first of these, a reading of Winters' poem "To the Holy Spirit," which appeared in *The Southern Review*, Autumn 1981, is an excerpt from the dissertation.

Finlay was devoted to the art of poetry. Everything else appeared to be secondary in his scale of values. He would go to great lengths to meet a poet he admired. He thought the syllabic poem "Still-Life" by the daughter of Robert Bridges, Elizabeth Daryush, was astonishingly beautiful, so off he went to meet her in her home on Boar's Hill, Oxford, England. Then he immediately returned to the States without bothering to see the sights of London.

In the seventies he became the nucleus of a group of four graduate students, all poets, who held similar views about the direction contemporary poetry should take. The other three are David Middleton, Wyatt Prunty, and Lindon Stall. They were writing good formalist verse a decade before today's much-heralded "New Formalists" appeared.

Broadly speaking, most of Finlay's poems fall into two categories—those derived from his personal experience as a southerner and as a student of southern history, and those derived from his fascination with ancient cultures. During the last ten years of his life he engaged in extensive readings in archaeology, Greek and Latin history, philosophy, and classical literature. Regardless of subject, his tone is usually somber and frequently tragic. The chief influence is probably

Yvor Winters and, like him, he usually employs a traditional prosody, a plain style devoid of complicated tropes, diction more denotative than connotative, with occasional violence reminiscent of another poet he admired, Allen Tate.

Among his most moving southern poems are "The Blood of Shiloh," a Confederate veteran's reminiscence of the mud and horror of battle worthy of Wilfred Owen; "The Wide Porch," on the death of Finlay's grandmother; "Audubon at Oakley," rich in vividly perceived descriptive detail; and "The Slaughter of the Herd," one of his last poems, which appeared in *The Classical Outlook,* Winter 1990-91. It is remarkable for its density of texture, its portrayal of the pastoral dream which ends in brutality and blood.

Of his poems dealing with ancient cultures one of the most interesting is "The Bog Sacrifice," which describes the discovery in Denmark of the well-preserved body of a hanged man probably sacrificed in a religious ritual two thousand years ago. Of this poem, Janet Lewis writes, "the form [metrical verse] supplies a lasting tranquility and gentleness to this old evidence of sacrifice, of the terror of divinity, acknowledged, accepted, come to terms with." "Ovid in Exile" is an appealing poem, the final lines of which undoubtedly express Finlay's own feeling of loneliness and isolation. There are at least a dozen other fine poems in this category. I am especially moved by the penultimate line of "The Last Act" which refers to the famous scene in *Antony and Cleopatra* when Hercules, to the sound of underground music, abandons Antony. The final lines read:

> The music underground,
> The quiet terror of its shifting source,
> Its echoes vanishing, is all that's left.

This departure of the gods from modern literature reminds me of Ezra Pound's "The Return," written over half a century ago, which deals with the approach of the gods to modern poetry—temporarily, according to Finlay.

In closing, I should mention another theme in Finlay's poetry—not obvious, but definitely there—that of Christian belief. It was present in the first poem I accepted from him in 1970 for *The Southern Review,* "Ash Wednesday," ten years before his conversion to Catholicism. It is there very movingly in the final stanza of one of his later poems, "The Autobiography of a Benedictine":

> Our mind is not some Virgil cursed
> To go back down to painful shades.

> Faith dies itself and is dispersed
> In minds the deathless Word pervades.

Finlay's poems are scattered among three volumes and several periodicals. There are a few still unpublished. A definitive annotated edition of his poetry is needed—and deserved.

Appendix J

"In Light Apart": The Achievement of John Finlay
by David Middleton (1999)[1]

> In light apart from me, I seek the Word
> Holding mind and blood from the absurd.
>
> ("The Fourth Watch")

In May of 1991, three months after John Finlay's death in February, I made the long sad journey from my home in Thibodaux, Louisiana, to the Finlay farm in Enterprise, Alabama, to begin my duties as Finlay's literary executor. In his one small room I found all he had left behind: his library, a few record albums, and his writings.

I had been encouraged by the response to my call for submissions of verse and prose for the small chapbook *A Garland for John Finlay,* which was published in November of 1990, just in time for Finlay, by then blind, to have the poems read to him one per day, which was all he had the strength to absorb. Through the *Garland,* Finlay came to know right at the end of his life just how highly he was regarded by so many fine English and American poets.

A number of those same poets are contributors to this Aldine Press book and special issue of *Hellas* devoted to John Finlay. A brief glance at the table of contents and the authors' page will confirm what both the *Garland* promised and what I myself suspected after long acquaintance with his works, published and unpublished: John Finlay has written verse and prose of lasting value including at least a handful of poems which are among the best short poems in measured verse in the American literary tradition.

All who admire Finlay's works are indebted to his publishers: Robert L. Barth, who published John's first two chapbooks and who continues his long, courageous commitment to provide an outlet for measured verse; Harry Duncan, who published John's third chapbook on his world-famous Cummington Press; John Daniel, who published Finlay's collected poems and his seminal book on Gnosticism and modernity; and now, Gerald Harnett, who has given me this opportunity to take the critical assessment of Finlay's life and work to a new level and to a wider audience with the publication of *In Light Apart: The Achievement of John Finlay.*

The essays printed here are not only fine studies in themselves but also suggest many directions in which the continuing discussion and evaluation of Finlay's works might go. At the very least we need an edition of Finlay's book-length study (his Ph.D. dissertation, 1980) of Yvor Winters' intellectual theism, an edition of the uncollected and unpublished prose (essays, reviews, diaries), the letters to and from Finlay, a critical biography, and a book-length study of the poems. The materials for most of these projects are in The John Finlay Papers now in the Lower Mississippi Valley Collections in the Archives of Hill Memorial Library at Louisiana State University in Baton Rouge. As Finlay's literary executor I stand ready to help any qualified scholar who is interested in taking on one or another of these tasks. The biography is perhaps the most urgently needed of these books while so many of those who knew Finlay best, both family and friends, are still alive.

I have often wondered, during these last seven years of my executorship, what it is about John Finlay that remains so compelling. For one thing, his life was emblematic: Finlay fought against what he saw as the demons of modernity while also being drawn to these same demons, almost against his will, on some deep level of his being. Finlay's literary works are thus at once objective studies of universal human concerns and a secret autobiography of his own profoundly personal struggles. Finlay's life and works are the story of this long battle which ended both in tragedy and triumph. The tragedy was the premature completion of his writing career at the beginning of his forty-ninth year and his death from AIDS at fifty. The triumph lies in the long campaign he waged both in the poetry and the prose in favor of an Aristotelian-Thomistic understanding of the world and against Gnosticism, relativism, narcissism, the horrors of modern war, and in his evocative depiction of what, in the title of a late chapbook of verse first published in the fall of 1997 by Robert L. Barth, he called *The American Tragedies*: the conflicts between whites, blacks, and Indians; the Civil War; and the dangerous illusion that America was somehow free from European history, if not history as a whole, and thus from the givenness of the human condition. Finlay's heritage as a Southern writer deeply influenced by Allen Tate was an essential part of these and other poems on American and Southern history.

And so, in the end, having devoted his life to studying the crisis of modern man against the background of the classical-Christian civilization which he strove his whole life to master and inherit, Finlay was able to leave behind both poems and essays that achieve that measure of wisdom which only the greatest writers leave us as their legacy—"wisdom like salt / Which our own minds can gather from the sea" as he put it in the late poem "The Symposium for Socrates." This unshaken faith in the ability of the human mind to know the truth and to express it in verse is captured in the magnificent closing lines of *"Origo mentis,"* Finlay's powerful poem on the "origin of the mind." The Western philosophical mind here speaks of its own full realization outside Athens under the plane trees by the river Ilissus, the scene of Plato's *Phaedrus,* in the years just before the tragedy of the Peloponnesian War:

> It was dense poems and Socratic light,
> My endless afternoon before the war.
> Shade of the plane made water underneath
> So cool at noon, and in the summer too.
> We waded in the stream and then lay back
> Upon the sloping bank. Cicadas sang
> Those monotones of music made with fire.

Yet in spite of having written such unforgettable verse, it was Finlay's fate to die without being able to enjoy that full degree of recognition to which his best work entitled him. Living in isolation on the family farm in southeastern Alabama from 1981 until his death ten years later, Finlay sometimes wrote of his situation, though he always did so with a firm faith in the ultimate success of the way he had chosen to live out his literary life. In a letter to me of 17 January 1984, he said: "I feel that we are all in this together, that we are each other's best and frequently only audience, that we really write only for God and for each other, and so I was happy you liked the book [*The Wide Porch and Other Poems,* 1984]." One month later to the day, he wrote to me again about a most welcome letter from a writer he deeply admired: "Janet Lewis wrote me about *The Wide Porch.* . . . she said she liked the book and her letter pleased me a great deal. We write in such isolation . . . that when we get just one letter about our poems we are extraordinarily pleased."

In light of these remarks, it is not surprising that a number of Finlay's finest poems deal with the figure of the isolated artist or thinker and his struggle to understand the world. One such artist who tried to bring together in his paintings of birds both the material reality of the creatures and an intellectual understanding of them is John James Audubon:

> I saw my book, taut wings of mockingbirds
> In combat with the snake knotted beneath
> The nest, its open mouth close to the eggs,
> Now held forever in the lean, hard line.
> And underneath, defining them, combined:
> The clean abstraction of their Latin names,

> The vulgate richness of this Saxon salt.
>
> ("Audubon at Oakley")

Then there is his poem about an old man reading the Bible by "sourceless light":

> Exposure salted his grave northern face.
> An unerasable sadness tinged that grace
> Of sourceless light glowing on solid form.
> Hard winter nights—the isolating storm—
> His oil burned out onto the living word.
> A man matured in loss, in griefs incurred
> By love outside himself, he would expend
> His mind on God, still opened to the end.
>
> ("On Rembrandt's Portrait of an Old Man
Reading the Scriptures")

Finally, there is his poem spoken by the exiled Ovid living out his life among barbarians. In their reference to that city which so readily stands as a symbol both of the classical and Christian worlds as well as of the modern world of letters, the poem's closing lines are surely autobiographical:

> And still I write—my muse alone inscribes
> Some peace, some reason on my lonely rage.
> I then am steeled to finish through my age.
> If Caesar should forbid me still my home,
> My death lies here. My poems live in Rome.
>
> ("Ovid in Exile")

It seems all but certain now that John Finlay's best poems and essays, in their heroic struggle to know the world as it really is, will "live in Rome" and there forever shine "in light apart."

Appendix K

Preface to *John Finlay: A Commemoration Upon the Occasion of the Twenty-Fifth Anniversary of His Death on February 17, 1991* (2016)[1]
by David Middleton

When Alabama poet John Finlay was approaching death in the fall of 1990, I promised him in a telephone conversation that I would see into print two books that he had completed in the 1980s while living on the family farm in Enterprise, Alabama. One book was published posthumously as *Mind and Blood: The Collected Poems of John Finlay* (1992). The other book was published as *Hermetic Light: Essays on the Gnostic Spirit in Modern Literature and Thought* (1994). Further publications by and about John Finlay are listed in the bibliography at the end of this chapbook.

After Finlay's death on February 17, 1991, I arranged for his papers to be placed in the Lower Mississippi Valley Special Collections at Louisiana State University where Finlay earned the Ph.D. in English in December of 1980. A note at the end of this chapbook describes these papers in more detail. Unless otherwise indicated, the poetry and prose herein will be found in The John Finlay Papers at LSU.

John Finlay: A Commemoration is intended to honor and remember Finlay upon the occasion of the twentieth-fifth anniversary of his death. This limited-edition chapbook is meant especially to be both a celebration and a consolation for John Finlay's surviving family and friends. It is also published to encourage scholars to make use of The John Finlay Papers—and other sources—to deepen our understanding and appreciation of Finlay's life, ideas, poetry, and prose. Work remains to be done, including a biography, an updated bibliography, a new edition of the poetry, and editions of the prose, especially the diaries and correspondence with important literary figures such as Edgar Bowers, Andrew Lytle, Donald E. Stanford, Lewis P. Simpson, Janet Lewis Winters, and others.

For an introduction to Finlay's life and writings, the reader should consult the bibliography and begin perhaps with my "Preface" to *Mind and Blood: The Collected Poems of John Finlay*, my "Afterword" to *Hermetic Light: Essays on the Gnostic Spirit in Modern Literature and Thought*, and Jeffrey Goodman's "The Romance of Modern Classicism: Remarks on the Life and Work of John Finlay (1941-1991)."

As one example of scholarly work that might yet be done on Finlay, I reprint below Finlay's last poem, "A Prayer to the Father." For the story of the composition of this poem in the last year of Finlay's life, see my essay "John: An Anglican Meditation on Literary Gifts and

Giving." There is some uncertainty as to whether Finlay intended, or would have seen as a helpful change, the use of commas before and after "fused together" in line 6. This poem, as dictated by Finlay and including the punctuation he wanted, was privately printed after his death as a memorial by the Finlay family. But a surviving copy of this original printing has been hard to find. Perhaps one day a copy—or other conclusive evidence—will emerge. Until then, the reader is invited to compare the version below with the version—without these commas—in *Mind and Blood*, a version typed out by myself in March of 1991 from the now missing original. In his poem "John," which opens his *Collected Poems* (1997), the distinguished American poet Edgar Bowers (1924-2000) called "A Prayer to the Father" "the poem that is his best."

A Prayer to the Father

Death is not far from me. At times I crave
The peace I think that it will bring. Be brave,
I tell myself, for soon your pain will cease.
But terror still obtains when our long lease
On life ends at last. Body and soul,
Which, fused together, should make up one whole,
Suffered deprived as they are wrenched apart.
O God of love and power, hold still my heart
When death, that ancient awful fact appears;
Preserve my mind from all deranging fears,
And let me offer up my reason free
And where I thought, there see Thee perfectly.

In response to my promise, noted above, to see his two books into print, John replied, "You'll have to be Bridges to my Hopkins." Like English poet Robert Bridges (1844–1930), who was the literary executor for his friend and fellow poet Gerard Manley Hopkins (1844–1889), I too became an executor—for John Finlay—who wrote an essay on Hopkins and who, like Hopkins, did not live to enjoy the full measure of fame that his best literary works certainly deserve. Finlay did live to receive *A Garland for John Finlay* (1990), a chapbook of poems by American and English poets who were admirers of Finlay's work.

I like to think that both Bridges and Hopkins would have valued the best of John Finlay's poetry, especially his final poem, printed above—Bridges for its plain, classical style and Hopkins for its theological subject matter.

The life of the mind and the craft of poetry meant nearly everything to John Finlay. Finlay pays homage to the writer as a central cultural figure in a poem he wrote at age twenty-one upon the occasion of the death of the internationally known southern novelist William Faulkner (1897–1962). The last line of the poem echoes Faulkner's Nobel Prize Speech delivered on December 10, 1950 in Stockholm, Sweden.

from "In Memory of William Faulkner"

died July, 1962

> We need our artists . . .
> . . . .
> They weave, the magic web of thought
> And remind us of things likely forgotten
> In times of hunger and evils—
> The old verities of the human heart.

A final note:

Except for "A Prayer to the Father," "The Wide Porch," and "Salt from the Winter Sea," the poems in this chapbook—all previously unpublished or uncollected—were written mainly during the years of Finlay's early maturity from the 1960s through the 1970s. They are presented, as best as can be determined at present, in chronological order and are published now as an important part of the record of Finlay's development as a poet. The reader should consult *Mind and Blood* (1992) for the great majority of the poems of Finlay's full maturity, the poems upon which his reputation will largely rest. The prose in this chapbook—most of it previously unpublished—shows Finlay both as a younger writer finding his way and also as a mature writer and thinker.

A few apparent errors in spelling, punctuation, word forms, omitted words, and other matters have been either silently corrected or noted in brackets.

—David Middleton, literary executor for John Finlay

February 2016

Appendix L

The Break-In, a poem on John Finlay by David Middleton

> How strange seeing your poems in a book. . . .
> I once could feel the pathos of those nights
> About them still in hottest Baton Rouge,
> Black coffee, poverty, the sweated line!
>
> —John Finlay (1941–91), "To a Friend on His First Book,"
> *Between the Gulfs* (1986)

Some forty years ago . . . yet in my mind
From time to time I see those rooms again—
That spare unshared apartment where you lived,
Earning the Ph.D. at LSU—
A bed half-made, a nightstand with its lamp,
Ash tray, and cigarettes, and on the floor
A stack of books you read, then underscored,
Engaging every text, intently fixed,
Your very being seemingly at stake,
Choragos in tense dialogue with kings,
From Holy Writ and Plato's Socrates
To Thomas, Dante, and the troubled reigns
Of Nietzsche, Freud, Tate, Kafka, Winters, James,
All actors in the drama of a soul
You strove to save from tragic turn and fall.

Your place had little more—a single pan
To heat up coffee-water on the stove,
A black typewriter with its sticky keys,
Long yellow pads for drafts of verse and prose,
Scenes from your struggles with the Gnostic gods
Then foreign to an Alabama farm
Whose seasons of the church and earth were one.

And there you'd dwelt among the things that tell—
Spring dogwoods, Easter lilies, hyacinths,
Late summer's morning glories, white and blue,
The fall's frost-aster petals on the ground,
And Christmas holly weaving winter peace

For mantel, yard, grave, chancel, garden, door,
Or pastures you would cross to reach a slope
With sisters watching as you called and traced
Between the primum mobile and pond
The northern constellations, name by name,
The Hunter and the Dragon and the Lyre—
Job's Coffin held aloft by dark and stars.

Sometimes that realm could seem so far away
And yet be near "in hottest Baton Rouge"
Where you walked back one night to quiet rooms
From wine and conversation, new work shared
Through dinner with likeminded poet friends
To spy a door ajar, a window prized
By thieves who'd broken in but then had found
Nothing worth stealing—old clothes, older books,
A manual Underwood, fair-copies typed,
Ashes of finished cigarettes and thoughts,
No TV, radio, hi-fi, or cash—
And so fled empty-handed, cursing God.

And when you saw that all you had was there—
The cinder-block bookshelves' unpainted boards
Still holding Shakespeare, Milton undisturbed—
A poor man dancing past the robber band,
You knew you had been faithful to a gift
The Holy Ghost as Muse bestowed at birth,
Plowing by mind and hand down lines and rows,
True to the ancient sanctions of the land.

And though in your own way you'd come to drink
Like Socrates the poison of the age—
Narcissus leaning breathless to the pool,
Sherlock aroused for Moriarty's kiss—
You wrote late poems and essays to be whole,
Returning to that place where you were born,
Full harvests of a blood moon in the fields
As you stayed up all night, suffering AIDS
A decade while completing those two books,
Your story left for others who would strive
For mind's integrity, which, years ago,
A break-in had confirmed, exemplified,
As did your final moment's final breath

When from your deathbed halfway rising up,
With blinded eyes you looked beyond and said
"Plato?" to one now sent to take you home
To that last, great symposium of Love
At which the conversation never ends.

Notes

Mind and Blood: The Collected Poems of John Finlay
(original version; late 1980s)

The Wide Porch and Other Poems (1984)

1. M.C.F. is Mattie Coston Finlay (1887–1976), John Finlay's paternal grandmother. Within the family, she was known as "Ma." Finlay's sister, JoAnn Finlay Hall, writes, "John was the first grandchild and all through life was close to her." Hall says of the house in this poem, "My great-grandfather built it. MaMa [Toxey Ard Sorrell, Finlay's maternal grandmother] said all the men in the town helped each other build their homes with what they could do. My great-grandmother had seven children. MaMa inherited the house because she lived there with her four children, because her husband died early in the mental institution. The house had sixteen rooms. We spent many fun times swinging on the front porch and playing from the balcony upstairs." In his important bio-critical essay on Finlay, Jeffrey Goodman comments on the significance of this poem: "'I then moved outward to become myself,' Finlay wrote in 'The Wide Porch,' the first poem in his first book. From a biographical perspective, he was saying: when, on any occasion, I moved outward from Enterprise, it symbolized a parallel growth in the poetic mind. When Finlay bade farewell to the farm community of Enterprise for the university town of Tuscaloosa in September 1959, he carried his provincial values with him, like Aeneas his household gods. Oddly, Finlay's provincial values had a great deal in common with classical values: his father's capacity for intense, sustained work; his mother's family and friends' culture of mind; and the Baptist and Methodist faith of his ancestors." "The Romance of Modern Classicism: Remarks on the Life and Work of John Finlay, 1941–1991," *The Alabama Literary Review*, 14:2, Fall 2000, 27–28.

2. Established in the nineteenth century, Margaret Claybank Cemetery is near Ozark, Alabama. Members of John Finlay's family are buried at Claybank. The uncle is Uncle Waldo Ard. Claybank Church—built of logs in 1852 to replace a similar church house constructed in 1829-30 by original settlers in the Claybank

area—still stands. Granite headstones for some members of the extended Finlay family buried at Claybank have surging waves. JoAnn Finlay writes, "Claybank is the church founded by relatives and other settlers moving to Dale County from South Carolina. When visiting Ozark [from Enterprise], it was always to go with MaMa and Uncle Waldo to clean the family plot." Hall adds: "John is buried in the Finlay plot at Meadowlawn Cemetery in Enterprise."

3. "In the Adriatic" is a post-symbolist poem. As defined by Yvor Winters in "The Post-Symbolist Methods," Chapter V, in *Forms of Discovery*, (Chicago: Alan Swallow, 1967), 251–297, a post-symbolist poem uses controlled associationism, that is to say, the poem realistically describes a scene whose details suggest specific (not vague and indefinite) ideas and feelings. In this poem Finlay depicts the fragility of even long established human civilization (the old groves of deeply rooted olive trees) as seen against the background of an ever changing and threatening natural order (the black water pulling at the base of the rock). For more on Finlay and Winters, see Note 12 below.

4. The probable scene in this poem is recalled by JoAnn Finlay Hall: "I believe this to be an old fishing camp/bar located between Panama City, Florida, and Fort Walton [Beach], Florida. It is on the bay and I know John went there." In a letter of November 14, 1971, to Donald E. Stanford—poet, critic, scholar, editor of *The Southern Review*, and Finlay's major professor for doctoral studies at Louisiana State University—Finlay wrote: "All three of you [Stanford, Emily Dickinson, and Wallace Stevens] in one way or another deal with the natural world that no longer has the benefit of the Christian vision. And your 'universe' is so like Stevens'—beautiful, mysterious, and always there." The John Finlay Papers, Louisiana State University.

5. These lines are spoken by the Second Soldier in William Shakespeare's play *Antony and Cleopatra*, Act 4, Scene 3, 21–22. Hercules was Antony's patron god.

6. Ash Wednesday is the first day of Lent, the season of fasting, self-examination, repentance, and self-denial. At Ash Wednesday services, the priest takes ashes and makes a cross on the forehead of each worshipper at the altar rail saying, "Remember, man, that thou art dust, and unto dust thou shalt return." Finlay's poem shows the tension within himself between mind and blood as in

the title of his collected poems.

7. The source of details in this poem is *The Bog People: Iron Age Man Preserved* by Danish archaeologist P.V. Glob (1911–85). Finlay used the 1969 English translation, published in America by Ballantine Books. At the bottom of a copy of the poem sent to David Middleton, Finlay added the following: "A NOTE: The subject of this poem is a composite figure of several of the bog-men discovered during the 1950's in Denmark, the account used being that of P.V. Glob, *The Bog People.* The goddess, for whom these men died, is one of fertility; a contemporary account of her is found in Tacitus' *Germania*." "The Bog Sacrifice" describes the human sacrifice in pre-Christian Denmark of a young man to this fertility goddess. Glob's conclusion to *The Bog People* may dramatically intensify a reader's reaction to the line in Finlay's poem "Before Christ reached this isolated north." Glob writes as follows: "The Tollund man and many of the other bog men, after their brief time as god and husband of the goddess—the time of the spring feasts and the wanderings through their villages—fulfilled the final demand of religion. They were sacrificed and placed in the sacred bogs; and consummated by their death the rites which ensured for the peasant community luck and fertility in the coming year. At the same time, through their sacrificial deaths, they were themselves consecrated for all time to Nerthus, goddess of fertility—to Mother Earth, who in return so often gave their faces her blessing and preserved them through the millennia" (132). By contrast, in Christian belief, Christ's death on the cross was the one necessary and sufficient sacrifice for the sins of humankind. Jeffrey Goodman has offered this commentary on the poem: "A poem entitled 'The Bog Sacrifice' nicely illustrates Finlay's mature art. Written soon after his return from Europe, it is Finlay's first major success. Based on *The Bog People*, a popular study of northern European primitives that also inspired the Irish poet Seamus Heaney, it tells the tale of the exhumed, preserved body of an Iron Age boy sacrificed one spring to the chthonic goddess of the under earth. Its classical subject is the sacrifice of the boy to tribal needs, life to idea. The boy's experience is presented from the outside, objectively, yet fully felt inside, subjectively. Its modern voice freshens this classical concern as well as any poem Finlay wrote. The poem is aesthetic *and* moral repairing the nineteenth century's deep and vicious laceration between the two experiences." "The Romance of Modern Classicism: Remarks on the Life and Work of John Finlay, 1941–1991," *The Alabama*

Literary Review, 14:2, Fall 2000, 40.

8. Narcissus was a beautiful young man, the son of Cephissus (a river god) and Liriope (a water nymph). In one telling of the myth, Narcissus rejected the love of Echo (a mountain nymph) and fell in love with his own reflection in a pool. He stared at his refection until he pined away and died. Finlay's "Narcissus in Fire" applies this myth to modern solipsism. Andrew Littauer has said of this poem: "The imagery of the poem suggests a self-made hell that can occur with too dangerous a degree of self-critical introspection and life-denying introversion. . . . But it is never made clear whether the 'anguish' is a matter of guilt or is induced by something else altogether. The poem is spectral and elusive. The title, however, gives to the poem its particular spin. This hell-haunted figure has allowed himself to lapse into an insidious kind of intellectual introversion and self-absorption." "Mind and the Classical World in the Poetry of John Finlay." *In Light Apart: The Achievement of John Finlay*. Edited by David Middleton (Glenside, PA: The Aldine Press, 1999), 167.

9. Hannah Arendt (1906–1975), born in Germany, was an American political philosopher. The quotation is from the "Introduction" to her book *On Revolution* (1963): "Cain slew Abel, and Romulus slew Remus; violence was the beginning and, by the same token, no beginning could be made without using violence, without violating. The first recorded deeds in our biblical and our secular tradition, whether known to be legendary or believed in as historical fact, have travelled through the centuries with the force which human thought achieves in the rare instances when it produces cogent metaphors or universally applicable tales. The tale spoke clearly: whatever brotherhood human beings may be capable of has grown out of fratricide, whatever political organization men may have achieved has its origin in crime. The conviction, in the beginning was a crime—for which the phrase 'state of nature' is only a theoretically purified paraphrase—has carried through the centuries no less self-evident plausibility for the state of human affairs than the first sentence of St. John, 'In the beginning was the Word,' has possessed for the affairs of salvation." Related to this poem is Finlay's essay "Three Variations on the Killing of the Father: Nietzsche, Freud, and Kafka" in the companion volume of Finlay's collected prose: *"With Constant Light": The Collected Essays and Reviews Along with Selections from the Diaries, Letters, and Other Prose of John Martin Finlay (1941–1991)*. Edited by David

Middleton and John P. Doucet. Belmont, NC: Wiseblood Books, 2020, pages 113-130.

10. The story of the "father" in "The Black Earth" is based, to some extent, on Finlay's strained relationship with his own father, Tom Coston Finlay (1918–1983), who had to take over working his family's farm at age sixteen. JoAnn Finlay Hall says, "No doubt he loved us, but [found it] difficult to express [that love]." According to Finlay's mother, Jean Sorrell Finlay, her son John told her near his death, "Mama, I have finally made my peace with Daddy." In a letter of February 4, 1982, to Lewis P. Simpson, the renowned scholar of American literature and editor of *The Southern Review*, Finlay wrote of "The Black Earth": "Here I am again. I've worked and worked on this poem and hope I have it in good enough shape for you. You have another version which I think is a little too loose and un-concentrated. I cut out two stanzas and changed some here and there. I guess I'm worried about it because of its psychological disclosure, but I mean the 'constant light' at the end to take it out of an exclusive Freudian context where its bluntness might put it for some readers. Or at least I hope it does. But enough of it. I never want to see the thing again. I can't remember the deadline you gave me last spring, but I hope I'm in time." The John Finlay Papers, Louisiana State University.

11. In a letter to David Middleton of April 9, 1982, Finlay wrote of this poem: "Here is a copy of the poem I just finished. The title comes from the sea-walking passage in St. Matthew: 'And in the fourth watch he came to them, walking on the sea.' I got the first stanza by thinking about the aesthetics of Mallarmé and Wallace Stevens; the argument in the fourth stanza is pretty compressed— does it work? Let me know what you think of it. As I said to you on the phone, I feel very close it, so close in fact, that criticism wouldn't upset me at all." Private collection of David Middleton. The poem begins—in its epigraph—with a miracle, the calming of the waters of the sea, and ends both with another water miracle, that of the water being turned into wine at the wedding at Cana.

12. Yvor Winters (1900–1968) was an American poet and literary critic who had a profound influence on Finlay. Born in Chicago, Winters was a doctoral student and then a professor of English at Stanford University from 1927 until his retirement in 1966. Winters' earlier poems are in free verse, but in the late 1920s he turned to traditional measured verse. Donald E. Stanford, poet,

professor of English, editor of *The Southern Review* at Louisiana State University, and a student of Winters, summed up Winters' views on poetry in his book *Revolution and Convention in Modern Poetry* (Newark, NJ: University of Delaware Press, 1983, 193): "Winters' position . . . was that a satisfactory poem should have a rationally defensible paraphrasable content—but that this paraphrasable content was by no means the total meaning of the poem. The total meaning of the poem included the effective use of rhythm and other poetic devices which qualify and convey the paraphrasable content to the reader." Finlay wrote to Stanford in December of 1969 asking him to be his major professor for a proposed course of study of Winters and of poets associated with Winters. That letter is published in *"With Constant Light": The Collected Essays and Reviews Along with Selections from the Diaries, Letters, and Other Prose of John Martin Finlay (1941–1991)*, page 243. Finlay's dissertation, completed in 1980 at LSU, is entitled "'The Unfleshed Eye': A Study of Intellectual Theism in the Poetry and Criticism of Yvor Winters." The details in "Odysseus" are drawn from Homer's *The Odyssey*, Books V–VIII. Finlay's "Odysseus" can be read as a statement of Finlay's Wintersian poetics.

13. The "blind poet" is Demodocus, court poet of King Alcinous of the Phaeacians with whom Odysseus stays a while on his journey home to Ithaca. Demodocus sings of the fall of Troy, the story of which has preceded Odysseus' arrival in Phaeacia, and Odysseus is deeply moved by this song. Jeffrey Goodman writes of Finlay's time on Corfu and this poem: "Corfu was purported to be the mythic island of Phaeacia where Odysseus visited King Alcinous. There he listened with high wonder as the rhapsode sang of the hero's past adventures. This no doubt attracted Finlay strongly. A propos, he began the brief persona poem 'Odysseus' (in honor of Yvor Winters) by saying 'I could not know the meaning of that time / . . . Until I heard the voyage beat out in words.'" "The Romance of Modern Classicism: Remarks on the Life and Work of John Finlay, 1941–1991," *The Alabama Literary Review*, 14:2, Fall 2000, 38. The poems "Odysseus" and "Audubon at Oakley" originally appeared in *The Southern Review*, Spring 1982, 18:2, 356–57, under the overall title "Two Poems in Memory of Yvor Winters."

14. Archaic Athena: Athena, the daughter of Zeus, was the divine protector of Athens and the goddess of wisdom, the arts and crafts, and warfare. Finlay's poem is apparently based on a

rural shrine—perhaps the Sanctuary of Athena Pallenis—but also possibly recalling details from the early history of the Old Temple of Athena on the Acropolis in Athens. Sometime in the mid 1970s, Finlay joined David Middleton for supper at Pinetta's, a restaurant in Baton Rouge. Finlay had just finished composing "The Archaic Athena" and wrote out a copy for Middleton, from memory, on a restaurant napkin.

15. John James Audubon (1785–1851) was a naturalist and painter, most famous for his color plates in *The Birds of America* (1827–38). Audubon spent time in Louisiana from 1821 through 1837. While tutor to the daughter of Lucretia Pirrie, who owned Oakley Plantation near St. Francisville, Audubon painted pictures of birds he discovered in the woods around Oakley. Finlay may have visited Oakley while a graduate student at LSU in Baton Rouge. Finlay appended the following note to this poem: "Oakley was a plantation outside St. Francisville, Louisiana, where Audubon lived and worked during the summer and fall of 1821." Finlay had originally planned a longer poem on Audubon. To support himself while researching and writing this longer poem, Finlay sought financial assistance from the Mary Roberts Rinehart Foundation. That proposal is included in this volume as Appendix B, pages 183-185. "Audubon at Oakley" is a portrait of the kind of artist Finlay himself, as a poet, wanted to be. This matter is discussed above in the 1992 Preface to *Mind and Blood*, pages 26-27. The closing lines of Finlay's poem are based on Audubon's painting "The Mocking Bird" in *The Birds of America*. "Different species of snakes ascend to their nests, and generally suck the eggs or swallow the young; but on all such occasions, not only the pair to which the nest belongs, but many other Mocking-birds from the vicinity, fly to the spot, attack the reptiles, and, in some cases, are so fortunate as either to force them to retreat, or deprive them of life."—Audubon. A draft version of this poem appears on pages 164-165. Finlay's sister, Betty Finlay Phillips, still has a print of this painting, which her brother John had owned.

16. Finlay appended the following note to these poems: "The first Sappho and the Callimachus are translations. The others are original poems based on the material of each poet."

17. Archilochus was a Greek poet (ca. 680–645 B.C.) known for his caustic wit and metrical virtuosity. A native of the island of Paros, Archilochus participated in a battle against the Thracians on

Thasos and died in a fight on the island of Naxos. Thrace was a region in southeastern Europe whose inhabitants were sometimes characterized by the ancient Greeks and Romans as warlike barbarians.

18. Sappho (ca. 610—ca. 570 B.C.) was a Greek poet born on the island of Lesbos. She is best known for her love lyrics, some of which are considered to be—after her place of birth—"lesbian" in nature. To Sappho is attributed the invention of a poetic form named after her, the Sapphic stanza. Finlay's first Sappho poem is his translation of Sappho 16 (*Greek Lyric*, translated by D.A. Campbell, No. 142, The Loeb Classical Library, Cambridge: Harvard University Press, 1982, I), 66–67.

19. Callimachus (ca. 305—ca. 240 B.C.) was born in Greek Libya and worked at the Library of Alexandria. He is best known for his epigrams and other brief poems. He strongly disliked the epic and other kinds of longer poems. Finlay's epigram is a translation of lines in different parts of Callimachus' *Aetia*, Book I, Poem 1 ("Against the Telchines") wherein Callimachus' dislike of the epic is clearly seen: "(I know that) the Telchines, who are ignorant and no friends of the Muse, grumble at my poetry because I did not accomplish one continuous poem of many thousands of lines. . . . It is not mine to thunder; that belongs to Zeus." (*Callimachus: Aetia, Iambi, Hecale and Other Fragments*, translated by C.A. Trypanis, No. 421, The Loeb Classical Library, Cambridge: Harvard University Press, 1958), 4–7.

Between the Gulfs (1986)

20. Finlay grew up in south Alabama, not far from the Florida panhandle. Several of Finlay's poems are set on the Gulf including "First Emblems," "The Road to the Gulf," "Salt from the Winter Sea," and "At Some Bar on Laguna Beach, Florida." In an entry in his Paris diary for December 3, 1973, Finlay wrote "Florida . . . is almost my half-home." As seen above, Finlay's second chapbook (1986) is entitled *Between the Gulfs*.

21. *Origo mentis*: The Origin of the Mind. The voice is that of the western philosophical mind, speaking of its own life—its birth, development, and apotheosis. In a note on this poem in *Between the Gulfs* Finlay wrote the following: "The first stanza of *Origo mentis* refers to the post-Mycenaean immigration of the Greeks to Asia

Minor where the first recorded philosophical question was asked and its answer attempted. I concentrate on the coastal islands since I am following here Bruno Snell who in *The Discovery of the Mind* saw the archaic lyric poets as the forerunners of the philosophers. And so the 'island cities' of Sappho and Archilocus [are] not the continental Miletus of Thales and other philosophers. The last stanza uses the scene of Plato's *Phaedrus*." Reproduced here is the corrected version of these notes as found at the end of Finlay's hand-corrected copy of *Between the Gulfs*. In the 1994 one-fold four-page card of Finlay's "Notes for the Perfect Poem," the final seven lines of "*Origo mentis*" were reprinted with the following note by David Middleton: "The scene is that of Plato's *Phaedrus*; the voice is that of the Western philosophical mind reaching its apotheosis in the Socratic conversations that occurred outside Athens on the banks of the Illissus, with its plane trees, in the years just before the fall of Athens to Sparta in the Peloponnesian War (431–404 B.C.)."

22. Finlay said that the word "bastard" (line 1) was suggested by its use in David Middleton's poem "Genealogy" in his poetic sequence *Hesiod in Old Age*, first published in the chapbook *Reliquiae* (R.L. Barth Press, 1983), n.p.

23. These island cities are the home islands of Sappho (Lesbos) and Archilocus (Paros). But "*Origo mentis*" also reflects Finlay's knowledge of Pre-Socratic philosophers, who lived on the western coast of Asia Minor.

24. Some of the details in this closing stanza, such as the song of the cicadas, come from Plato's *Phaedrus*.

25. These two poems are based on the tragic story of King Oedipus of Thebes as presented by the Greek playwright Sophocles (ca. 496–ca. 406 B.C.) in his play *Oedipus Rex*. Disregarding the warnings of the blind prophet Tiresias, Oedipus insisted on finding out the identity of the murderer of King Laius of Thebes, only to discover that he had fulfilled an earlier prophecy given to him at the Oracle of Delphi that he would slay his father and marry his mother. Having unknowingly killed his father, Laius, Oedipus then becomes King of Thebes and marries his mother, Laius' widow, Queen Jocasta. Oedipus is overwhelmed by the shock of knowing what he had insisted on discovering, blinds himself, and leaves Thebes, no longer king. The Oracle of Delphi was dedicated to Apollo.

26. The line "In whom Apollo sunk those awful claws" probably refers to the prophecy, at Apollonian Delphi, that sank deep into Oedipus' mind. Perhaps, on some level, this line also contains a reference to the raven, a symbol of ill fortune. The bird was associated with Apollo, who turned its white feathers black when the bird reported to him that his lover, Coronis, had been untrue to him. Also, Oedipus solved the Riddle of the Sphinx. The Sphinx had the head of a man, but the body of a lion with its clawed feet.

27. The root meaning of the word "tragedy" in ancient Greek is "goat song." Explanations of this etymology and usage include the winning of a goat as a prize in a contest between tragedians as part of a festival in honor of Bacchus or the wearing of goat-skins by actors playing the role of satyrs—human in shape, but having the legs of a goat.

28. Poseidon sent a white bull from the sea to Minos, king of Crete, to signify Minos' right to be king. Instead of sacrificing the bull as Poseidon had wished, Minos kept it with his other cattle. Poseidon, in revenge, caused Minos' wife, Pasiphaë, to become enamored of the bull. Their union produced the Minotaur, half human and half animal.

29. "In Another Country": The title may recall Marlowe's *The Jew of Malta*, Act 5, Scene 14, 43–44; T.S. Eliot's use of those lines as an epigraph to his poem "Portrait of a Lady"; or Hemingway's short story "In Another Country." The poem is an encounter between Finlay, the well-read scholarly poet and essayist, and the man he might have been had he stayed at home and worked the family farm without getting an education.

30. "Holmes" of the poem's title is Sherlock Holmes, the London detective invented by Sir Arthur Conan Doyle (1859–1930) and the main character of numerous stories and several novels. Holmes is known for his use of logic and forensic evidence in solving cases. He sometimes injected drugs, perhaps cocaine or morphine, to relieve his boredom and calm his restless mind. Finlay was deeply impressed by English actor Jeremy Brett's portrayal of Holmes in *The Adventures of Sherlock Holmes* (Granada Television, 1984-94). Finlay saw something of himself in Holmes, especially as portrayed by Brett and as depicted in this poem.

31. The *"scientific searcher"* is Holmes' name for the kind of detective

he is ("The Adventure of Black Peter").

32. The *"great malignant brain"* ("The Adventure of the Norwood Builder") is that of Holmes' archenemy, Professor James Moriarty, whom Holmes called the "Napoleon of crime" ("The Adventure of the Final Problem").

33. Solon (ca. 630–ca. 560 B.C.) was an Athenian ruler, legal reformer, and poet. After his death, Solon came to be seen as a forerunner of a more democratic Athens. His laws included debt relief, citizenship for foreign-born artisans, and the creation of a political framework for more widespread participation in government, but neither the rich nor the poor were contented with Solon's reforms.

34. To insure their survival, Solon had his laws inscribed on tablets or pillars (*kyrbeis*) for public reading and preservation. Pisistratus and other tyrants ruled Athens after Solon.

35. The speakers of this poem are early European explorers sailing to the New World in search of gold, and, perhaps, the Earthly Paradise or New Eden. Finlay's poem describes what most of them found. In a letter to David Middleton of June 27, 1984, Finlay commented on this poem: "The Inferno comes out of past reading; an account of Darwin's first voyage, Prescott's *History of the Conquest of Peru*, and the Ulysses episode in Dante. I started to call it 'Beyond the Pillars of Hercules' or 'Outside the Central Sea'. But both sounded melodramatic."

36. The "old houses" are the Houses of the Zodiac.

37. The ceiba is a tree found in or near the tropics in the Americas. Its trunk has few if any limbs below its top, which is a large canopy.

38. A Judas Tree (*cercis silliquastrum*) is so named because of the belief that Judas hanged himself on such a tree, which is native to Western Asia. The Judas Tree flowers in spring and produces deep pink blossoms. In a letter to David Middleton of January 14, 1985, Finlay commented on "The Judas Trees": "I'm enclosing a new poem of my own, one that was written in just one week, a recklessly abbreviated time for me. It comes out of my past. A composite of some Southern Medeas whom I knew long ago is intended. I tried to loosen up the iambic line here and there. In fact, I at first wanted to do it in accentual meter, but the old

never-to-be-forgotten pull of the iambic was too strong. I really don't know what I think of it, or even if I should think about it, and so will appreciate your reaction to it." Private collection of David Middleton. The closing lines of the poem may allude to the dangerous female sea monster Scylla whose voice was like the yelp of a dog and who "had a girdle of dogs' heads about her loins." *The Oxford Classical Dictionary*. 2nd edition. Edited by N.G.L. Hammond and H.H. Scullard. Oxford: Clarendon Press, 1970. 968.

39. Virgil (70–19 B.C.), the famous Roman poet, was the author of the epic poem *The Aeneid*. The poem recounts the battle of Troy in which the Greeks take and burn the city; the wanderings and adventures of the Trojan hero Aeneas and his followers; and Aeneas' establishment of a new Trojan civilization in Italy in the region where Rome was founded. Especially after the American Civil War, southerners would identify with the Trojans in Virgil's account of the fall of Troy and would see the Yankees as the Greeks who burned cities in the South, such as Columbia, South Carolina. The woman addressed in "The Judas Trees" is a contradiction. She believes in the southern myth of Confederates as Trojans and Yankees as Greeks yet has lived, in a kind of Judas-like betrayal, in accordance with the values of modernity, which the Union victory in the Civil War—at least in the minds of some southerners—insured. Finlay would have found this myth in the poetry of Allen Tate (1899–1979). In his "Aeneas at Washington," Tate has Aeneas journey not to Italy but to Washington, D.C. Aeneas sees the Capitol as a symbol of modernity and thinks, in contrast, of Troy: "I stood in the rain, far from home at nightfall / By the Potomac, the great Dome lit the water. / The city my blood had built I knew no more / While the screech-owl whistled his new delight / Consecutively dark. // Stuck in the wet mire / Four thousand leagues from the ninth buried city / I thought of Troy, what we had built her for." And in "To the Lacedemonians," an old Confederate veteran says to his fellow soldiers: " . . . we shall not fight again / The Yankees with our guns well-aimed and rammed— / All are born Yankees of the race of men / And this, too, now, the country of the damned[.]"

40. Finlay loved the poem "Still-Life" by English poet Elizabeth Bridges Daryush (1887–1977), daughter of English poet laureate Robert Bridges (1844–1930). In September of 1969, Finlay flew to England in order to meet Daryush at her home outside Oxford

and express his admiration for her poetry. (See Finlay's notes on this visit in the Wiseblood Books companion volume of his prose, *"With Constant Light": The Collected Essays and Reviews Along with Selections from the Diaries, Letters, and Other Prose of John Martin Finlay (1941–1991)*, page 240. A fine essay on the relationship between Daryush's poem "Still-Life" and Finlay's "A Room for a Still Life" is Glenn Bergeron's "John Finlay's 'A Room for a Still Life' and Elizabeth Daryush's 'Still-Life'" in *In Light Apart: The Achievement of John Finlay* (Glenside, PA: The Aldine Press, 1999), 178–83. These two poems are in the tradition of the ekphrastic poem, a poem based on a work of art (such as a "still life"), though in both cases here the antecedent "still life" picture or picture-like scene seems to have been invented by the poet.

41. Finlay is using "pelagic" (metaphorically) as meaning the open waters of the seas or oceans.

42. Finlay added the following note to this poem in *Between the Gulfs* (1986): "*Death in Asia Minor* is largely based on Aelius Aristides' *Sacred Teachings*, which I first learned about in E.R. Dodd's *Pagan and Christian in an Age of Anxiety*. The practice referred to in the poem is *incubation*, the staying overnight in a sacred place in order to receive some special communication from the god concerned. The bloodletting with which the poem ends must not be conceived as taking place inside the temple, but in some adjacent building, since the spilling of blood was considered a profanation and would have been prohibited on consecrated ground even if, as in this case, it had been dictated by the god himself."

43. Kerkera (Kerkyra) is Corfu, a Greek island in the Ionian Sea. Finlay spent parts of 1972 and 1973 on this island and kept a diary during his time there. See *"With Constant Light": The Collected Essays and Reviews Along with Selections from the Diaries, Letters, and Other Prose of John Martin Finlay (1941–1991)*, pages 255-257 for Corfu diary entries. Poems based on his experiences on Corfu include "At Kerkera," "Kalámai," and "Dunescape with a Greek Shrine."

44. The friend is Louisiana-born poet Lindon Stall (1948—). The book referred to is Stall's chapbook *Responsoria* (Florence, KY: R.L. Barth Press, 1983). Finlay and Stall met in Baton Rouge in 1970 while both were graduate students in English at Louisiana State University. Lines for a possible revision of this poem appear on pages 260-261, Note 92 and Note 93.

45. Of "The Dead and the Season" JoAnn Finlay Hall writes, "This poem is about our father's brother, Uncle Duncan. He and our father were total opposites, and John would be more like him [Duncan]. He was in the Army and Ma asked him to come home to farm. He was not a farmer and a car hit his tractor killing him. I remember him dying in the hospital with blood on the pillow."

The Salt of Exposure (1988)

46. The actor is Ronald Wilson Reagan (1911–2004), the fortieth president of the United States (1981–89).

47. Ovid (43 B.C.–17/18 A.D.) is the Roman poet and author of collections of poems such as *Amores* and *Metamorphoses*. He was banished from Rome in 8 A.D. by Augustus Caesar. Ovid claimed that his banishment was the result of a poem and an indiscretion, both unnamed, but the poem may have been the *Ars Amatoria*. Ovid's place of exile was Tomis, a city on the Euxine (Black) Sea. There he lived among the Getae, who spoke no Latin. Ovid wrote many poems in exile such as *Tristia*, begging to be allowed to return to Rome and to his family there, but Ovid died in exile. In a letter of January 23, 1987, Finlay sent this poem in couplets and others to Donald E. Stanford for criticism. Finlay says "the poems themselves are rather bleak in subject matter; I wish, of course, it were otherwise, but we all have to write what we have to write. I have been reading a lot of Dryden lately, a fact which explains my attempt, and experimentation, with the couplet which I am liking more and more." The other poems included with this letter are "The End of the Affair" (also in couplets), "The Blood of Shiloh," and "A Memory of the Frontier." In the copy enclosed with the letter, "Ovid in Exile" is entitled "The Exile of Ovid." The John Finlay Papers, Louisiana State University.

48. The Bear-Star is the northern constellation the Greater Bear.

49. Ister is an early name for the Danube River.

50. Mars was the Roman god of war.

51. "Rome" was, for Finlay, probably not only Ovid's Rome, but also Rome as the Eternal City and as a symbol of the Republic of Letters to which all writers belong and in which they hope their works will live on after their deaths. Finlay's early diary entries

for December of 1973 just after his arrival in Paris record his hopes that Paris would be his "intellectual home," something like Ovid's Rome. See *"With Constant Light": The Collected Essays and Reviews Along with Selections from the Diaries, Letters, and Other Prose of John Martin Finlay (1941–1991)*, pages 257-266, especially the entry for December 3, 1973. By 1974, however, Finlay was back home in Alabama writing to himself in another diary entry, "You must make a Paris in your own mind." Finlay's own death lay seventeen years off, not in Paris or in Rome, but in rural south Alabama. Finlay probably saw something of himself and his own life in Ovid, so the closing lines of this poem are, in one sense, autobiographical.

52. Henry James (1843–1916) is the highly regarded American novelist who spent most of his adult life in Europe, mainly in England. He often wrote of the complex relationships between Europeans and Americans. He became a British citizen in 1915 and was awarded the Order of Merit by King George V in 1916, the year of his death.

53. The *"distinguished thing"* was death, whose nearness became apparent on December 1, 1915, when James suffered a stroke. James' biographer Leon Edel recounts the scene in London: "The pen literally dropped from his hand. The next morning, December 2, James's servants in his flat in Carlyle Mansions, Chelsea, heard him calling. It was 8:30 A.M. and James's left leg had given way under him as he was dressing. He was a very heavy man, and with difficulty Burgess and the maid got him into bed. The novelist was fully conscious. He was reported later to have told his friend Howard Sturgis that his thought as he collapsed was, 'So here it is at last, the distinguished thing.'" Leon Edel, "The Deathbed Notes of Henry James," *The Atlantic Monthly*, June 1968, 221.6. 103–05. James died on February 28, 1916, in his flat in Chelsea, London. He was deeply affected by what he lived to know of the carnage of the Great War (1914–18).

54. Descartes is René Descartes (1596–1650), the French philosopher and mathematician most widely known for his statement *"cogito ergo sum"* ("I think [or: reflect], therefore I am") and for what has been named after him, "Cartesian dualism," the belief that mind and body are completely separate substances that can only interact with one another. Beginning in 1618, Descartes served in Holland in the army of Prince Maurice of Nassau. Descartes

later returned to France, but then lived in Holland again from 1628 until 1649. In "Descartes in Holland," Finlay sees Cartesian dualism as related to modern relativism and solipsism wherein the mind can become locked within itself and, in essence, be severed not only from the body but also from the normal everyday world represented by the Dutch "burghers"—well-off, responsible, common-sense middle-class citizens of a town or borough. Compare the poems "Narcissus in Fire" and "The Faun" on pages 38 and 95 of this volume.

55. This fort is probably Fort Morgan, which the Finlay family feels fairly certain John Finlay visited. The fort is a pentagonal bastion at the mouth of Mobile Bay. Constructed between 1819 and 1833, Fort Morgan was named after Revolutionary War hero Daniel Morgan (1736–1802). The fort played a major role in the Civil War as it guarded Mobile Bay from Union attack and allowed Confederate blockade-runners to operate. The fort fell to Union troops in August of 1864. The United States government turned the fort over to the State of Alabama in 1946. It is preserved now as an historical site. However, since, in the poem's title, Finlay calls this fort a "Spanish" fort, the poem may also be based in some ways on a hilltop fort—originally named Fort San Carlos de Austria—that was built by the Spanish in 1698. Destroyed by the French in 1719, the fort was rebuilt (1787–97) by the Spanish as Fort San Carlos de Barrancas. Now part of the Pensacola Naval Station on Pensacola Bay, the fort was designated as a national historic landmark in 1960. Perhaps Finlay brought together details from both forts. In the poem, Finlay contrasts what might be called the human scale of pre-modern warfare (the cannons of the fort) with the modern naval planes that carry payloads capable of causing a level of destruction unknown to previous ages.

56. Dedicated on November 13, 1982, the Vietnam War Memorial was designed by architect Maya Lin. It is composed of two walls, meeting at an angle of 125 degrees. On these walls are etched, chronologically, the names of the dead and those still listed as missing in action. Made of black granite, the stone reflects the faces of those who look at the names cut into it. The wings of the Memorial point toward the Washington Monument and the Lincoln Memorial.

57. Johnson is Samuel Johnson (1709–1784) ("Dr. Johnson"), the

famous English man of letters known for his essays, poetry, and biographies and for being the author of *A Dictionary of the English Language* (1755). The English physician Dr. Thomas Lawrence (1711–1783) was born in Westminster. He practiced medicine in London and served for several years as President of the London College of Physicians. He was one of Johnson's personal physicians. Suffering first from angina (1773) and then from a stroke (1782), Lawrence retired to Canterbury where he died in 1783. Finlay's poem is a translation of "AD T.L. MD," which can be found in *The Yale Edition of the Works of Samuel Johnson, Volume 6, Poems*, edited by E.L. McAdam, Jr. with George Milne, New Haven, CT: Yale University Press. 1964, 298–99. Finlay's two Johnson translations first appeared in the chapbook *Samuel Johnson: Selected Latin Poems Translated by Various Hands* (edited by Bob Barth, Edgewood, KY: R.L. Barth Press, 1987), n.p.) In its 1995 edition, the chapbook has a dedication to two deceased contributors to the original 1987 edition: "in memory of John Finlay and Charles Gullans."

58. Johnson's poem *Summe Pater* is found on page 313 of the Yale Edition of *Poems*, along with the following note: "Johnson wrote this prayer during the night when a paralytic stroke temporarily left him unable to speak. On 19 June 1783 he wrote to [his friend] Mrs. Thrale about the attack, saying that he had composed the prayer in Latin verse 'that I might try the integrity of my faculties. ... The lines were not very good, but I knew them not to be very good: I made them easily, and concluded myself to be unimpaired in my faculties.'" The poem is given the title "Prayer on Losing the Power of Speech" in the Yale Edition. This poem may be compared to Finlay's final poem, "A Prayer to the Father," in *A Prayer to the Father,* page 94. In that poem Finlay pleads with God to leave his reason intact during the dying process so that the poet might freely "offer up" his reason to God after death when meeting God at last face to face.

59. The Battle of Shiloh occurred in southwestern Tennessee on April 6-7, 1862. It was the bloodiest battle up to that time in the Civil War. After initial success in an attack on the first day, the Confederates were forced back on the second day and retreated into northern Mississippi. Union casualties (dead and wounded) were over 13,000; Confederate casualties, over 10,000. Finlay's poem may be compared to "The Locked Wards" as a poem about madness and sanity. On March 12, 1987, Finlay wrote about

"The Battle of Shiloh" in a letter to Lewis P Simpson: "The poem is based on what my great-grandmother told me about her father. I hope I've got all the history right. I knew her in her extreme old age when she didn't quite have total control over her facts. She said once, for instance, that as a child, she put her head to the iron railing on the railroad and heard the cannon of the Battle of Mobile just then taking place." The John Finlay Papers, Louisiana State University. The Battle of Mobile Bay, August 5-23, 1864, resulted in a Union victory.

60. Snake Creek was one of the borders of the encampment of the Union troops. On the first day of the battle, Confederate forces overran some of the Union camps.

61. The Hornets' Nest was a name given to a field that ran beside a road called the Sunken Road. Union troops made a stand at the Hornets' Nest and endured withering fire from the Confederates, who eventually surrounded the Federals and forced a surrender of that position.

62. This poem is probably about American poet and scholar J.V. Cunningham (1911–85), long-time professor of English at Brandeis University. Cunningham is best known for his epigrams and other short poems written in traditional verse forms and in a plain, classical style, often with rhyme and sometimes with biting humor. Finlay was a great admirer of Cunningham's verse.

63. The word "Paraclete" is from the Greek (*parakletos*) and the Latin (*paracletus*) meaning advocate or comforter. In Christian theology, the Paraclete is the Holy Spirit.

64. Rembrandt van Rijn (1606–69) is the Dutch master painter. The likely painting upon which this poem is based is "Old Man Praying" (ca. 1661) in the Cleveland Museum Art. Its attribution to Rembrandt is now in dispute. Another source might be Rembrandt's "Philosopher in Meditation" (1632). A conflation of details from these two—or other—paintings by Rembrandt is also a possibility.

65. St. Benedict of Nursia (ca. 480–ca. 547) was a founder of monastic communities, the author of "The Rule of Saint Benedict," and the inspiration for the Order of Saint Benedict. Benedict called for moderation and balance in a monastic life of prayer and work (*ora et labora*) under an abbot. Finlay wrote in a letter to David

Middleton during a time when both poets were discouraged about success in their literary lives, "What are we to do but work and pray?" Jeffrey Goodman speculates that "'The Autobiography of a Benedictine' [is] derivative of J.V. Cunningham's translation of the twelfth-century Archpoet's *Confession*, both good poems." "*Mind and Blood*: An Introduction to the Poetry of John Finlay." *In Light Apart: The Achievement of John Finlay*. Edited by David Middleton (Glenside, PA: The Aldine Press, 1999), 29–30.

66. "Schools" refers to Medieval Scholasticism and its method of seeking and arguing for the truth of both general philosophical hypotheses and of dogmatic Christian teachings. It employed dialectical reasoning and disputation in argument and counter-argument by opponents on a set topic. It is possible that "Schools" also refers to the Schools of the Greek philosophers.

67. Horace (65–8 B.C.) was a Roman poet, a friend of Virgil, and a recipient of the largess of the wealthy patron Maecenas, who gave Horace the Sabine Farm which brought him happiness and which was a source of inspiration for his poetry. Horace is famous for his *Epodes, Odes, Satires*, and *Epistles*, including his epistle on the art of poetry, *Ars Poetica*. In the *Oxford Companion to Classical Literature* (Oxford: Oxford University Press, 1937; corrected version, 1969, 215), compiled and edited by Sir Paul Harvey, Harvey writes of Horace: "Horace's position as one of the greatest Roman poets rests on the perfection of his form, the sincerity and frankness of his self-portraiture, his patriotism, his urbanity, humor, and good sense. . . . Horace has been so universally read and admired that his influence on English poetry, both lyrical and satirical, is almost all-pervading."

68. Old Cock: Probably an ironic reference to the phallus as a kind of "god," but one whose urges no longer bother the aging monk.

69. The Porch of Solomon was most likely not a porch but a roofed and columned portico attached to the Temple in Jerusalem. On this Porch, Jesus taught at the Feast of the Dedication (John 10:23). After Christ's death, the Apostles preached there while "many signs and wonders were wrought among the people" (Acts 5:12).

70. Athena's grove: An olive grove sacred to Athena, goddess of wisdom, would probably represent to Finlay the classical equivalent to Benedictine moderation.

71. Virgil (70 B.C.–19 B.C.) is the Roman poet who wrote *The Eclogues, The Georgics,* and the epic poem *The Aeneid.* Finlay here refers to Virgil as a character in *The Divine Comedy* by medieval Italian poet Dante Aligheri (1265–1321). In Dante's poem, Virgil guides the character Dante through Hell (the *Inferno*) and Purgatory (the *Purgatorio*). However, as a pagan, even though a noble one, Virgil cannot enter Paradise (the *Paradiso*) through which Dante's beloved Beatrice is his guide. Virgil vanishes in Canto XXX of the *Purgatorio*. Also see Note 39 above.

72. The "deathless Word" refers to Christ as the divine Logos (Greek for "Word"), a coequal, pre-existent member of the Trinity along with God the Father and God the Holy Spirit. In Christian theology, Christ as Logos was the Creator of the cosmos.

73. JoAnn Finlay Hall said of "The Pastoral of the Primitives," "These recollections seem familiar [as being from] the early days [on the family farm] of no air conditioning. At night listening to sounds in the woods, seeing the cows flickering their tails and a big dinner at noon."

74. Of "Salt from the Winter Sea" JoAnn Finlay Hall writes, "This was a story told by Granny Coston about [how] as a young girl the men of the community would go on wagons to the Gulf of Mexico to gather salt. It was a long hard journey for them and they stayed camping on the beach. They probably went in November when there was a slack time from farming and [it] may have taken them into the winter to complete."

A Prayer to the Father (1992)

1. *A Prayer to the Father* was published as a chapbook in 1992 (Thibodaux, LA: Blue Heron Press). It was reprinted later that year as Section IV of *Mind and Blood*. The preface and the bibliography to this volume provide more information on this subject. The poems in *A Prayer to the Father* are all mature poems left behind unpublished at the time of Finlay's death in 1991. Just as Finlay had done in the three chapbooks published during his lifetime, so the editor of *A Prayer to the Father* tried to sequence the poems in this posthumous chapbook so as to achieve that additional level of significance beyond that of each poem taken individually.

2. This poem's title and first line recall Chaucer's line "Go litel book,

go, litel myn tregedie" in Book 5, line 1786 of *Troilus and Creseyde* (mid 1380s) and Spenser's "Goe little booke" in the poem "To His Booke," the prefatory poem to *The Shepheardes Calendar* (1579). With such poems or lines, poets send their work into the world, usually with a mixture of anxiety and hope concerning the work's reception. Finlay's poem adds an ironic twist to this tradition.

3. This poem was dictated by Finlay to his sister Betty in the spring of 1990 when Finlay was too ill to hold a pen and knew he was dying. He composed the poem in his head as his death poem. It was the last poem he wrote. JoAnn Finlay Hall recalls that her brother John "was bedridden at this time and could barely see. [My sister Betty Finlay Phillips] said he was adamant about how she was writing and phrasing the sentences [lines] and had to read out each beginning and ending of the sentence [line]."

4. "The Faun," probably composed in the early to mid 1970s, shows Finlay's maturation as a poet. He came back to this poem and mined it for ideas and lines for several later poems.

5. *"Est-ce en ces nuits sans fonds que tu dors et t'exiles"?*—Rimbaud, *Le Bateau ivre"* This line is from the book by French poet Arthur Rimbaud (1854–91). Its title translates as *The Drunken Boat* (written 1871–73; published 1884). The line Finlay uses here as an epigraph may be translated "Do you sleep, are you exiled, in those bottomless nights?" (*The Drunken Boat*, line 86).

6. Kalámai is the older name for Kalamata, a city in southern Greece on the Peloponnese peninsula.

7. The title refers to *Illuminations*, a series of prose poems by French poet Arthur Rimbaud (composed 1873–75, published 1886). Of Finlay's poem, Catharine Savage Brosman, the distinguished scholar of French literature and American poet, has written: ". . . the poem 'The *Illumination* of Arthur Rimbaud' presents in concise form the external and internal illumination (here I use the word ironically, as, presumably, Finlay did), of Rimbaud's destiny in Africa, during which he contracted cancer of the knee (complicated by syphilis), leading to amputation, and, not long after, death. The expression 'hermetic light' in the poem has multiple resonances. Somewhat oxymoronic, since one of the meanings of *hermetic* or 'relating to or characterized by occultism or abstruseness'—that is, what is not well-lit—it points not only to the magical, semi-Gnostic tradition of Hermes Trismegistus,

with its occult knowledge, but also to Rimbaud's prose poems *Les Illuminations*, with the double reference of 'painted plates' (illustrations) and 'mystical or supra-sensory visions.' Reinforcing the poem's title, 'hermetic light' suggests the limits of the negative 'illuminations' afforded by experience to the French prodigy (somewhat as in Flaubert in the 'brutal moonlight' [in Finlay's poem 'Flaubert in Egypt']); failure of 'artificial paradises' (drugs), of aberrant sexuality, of rebellion, of poetry, of all sorts of visions and evasions, failure even of the escape to Africa and its radical rejection of his brilliant literary past. This personal catastrophe, viewed by Finlay as symptomatic of the entire nineteenth century and its false gods, is projected by the poem onto the century that Rimbaud would not live to see, the 'time of the assassins,' when 'hermetic light' (here, the negation of the good, the embrace of evil) became realized in mass destruction." "John Finlay's French Illumination." In *Light Apart: The Achievement of John Finlay*. Edited by David Middleton (Glenside, PA: The Aldine Press, 1999), 154–55.

8. French poet Charles Baudelaire (1821–67) moved from Paris to Brussels in 1864, hoping to sell the rights to his literary works in Belgium. He smoked opium and drank heavily. In 1866 he had a serious stroke followed by paralysis and aphasia. He died in Paris in 1867.

9. *L'automne déjà!*—Rimbaud, *Une Saison en Enfer*. The words, which translate "Autumn already!," are from "Adieu," the last section of *A Season in Hell* (1873).

10. Flaubert's experiences in Egypt during a tour of the Middle East (1849-50.) are the subject of Finlay's essay "Flaubert in Egypt," in *"With Constant Light": The Collected Essays and Reviews Along with Selections from the Diaries, Letters, and Other Prose of John Martin Finlay (1941–1991)*, pages 35-46, the Wiseblood Books companion volume of Finlay's prose. In a letter of January 30, 1982, Finlay wrote to David Middleton: "My recent immersion in Flaubert makes me acutely sensitive to the value of . . . luminous, specific details, which really do the work for you if you let them alone and give them their own area of resonance and breathing room. That's the wonderful thing about them, isn't it?" Private collection of David Middleton. The phrase "luminous, specific detail" may be an echo of an essay by the modernist American poet Ezra Pound (1885–1972): "The artist seeks out the luminous

detail and presents it. He does not comment." Ezra Pound, "I Gather the Limbs of Osiris," *The New Age*, December 7, 1911, reprinted in *Ezra Pound: Selected Prose: 1909–1965*. Edited by William Cookson. New York: New Directions 1973, 23. Finlay's poetics includes but is not limited to Pound's doctrine of the luminous detail.

11. "A Flaubert fishing by obstinate isles—" echoes Section I of the poem *Hugh Selwyn Mauberley* (1920) by Ezra Pound (1885–1972): "His true Penelope was Flaubert, / He fished by obstinate isles; / Observed the elegance of Circe's hair / Rather than the mottoes on sun-dials." The phrase *"fleurs du mal"* (flowers of evil) refers to Baudelaire's book of poems *Le Fleurs du mal* (1857). The line "A house lit blue by TV screen at night" may be linked to an incident recorded by Glenn Bergeron: "I have heard another story which reports that Finlay once picked up the one television he had owned and disposed of it in a dumpster, frustrated with TV as a medium of communication altogether." "John Finlay and Gustave Flaubert: A Kinship of Artists," 8. Unpublished essay. Used with permission.

12. Finlay worked at Bryce Hospital in Tuscaloosa, Alabama in 1974. "The Locked Wards" is based on Finlay's observations of mental patients in Bryce, whose original name, when founded in 1861, was the Alabama State Hospital for the Insane. Finlay kept a journal in which he made many notes about these patients. Passages from this journal *The Orange Journal* appear in *"With Constant Light": The Collected Essays and Reviews Along with Selections from the Diaries, Letters, and Other Prose of John Martin Finlay (1941– 1991)*, pages 266-267. JoAnn Finlay Hall writes the following concerning this poem: "Bryce was the state mental institution located in Tuscaloosa. Our grandmother's husband, Warren Martin Sorrell, went there in his 30's and died there. It was always very hushed about as my grandmother never talked about him. They had four small children and she went home to live with her mother in Ozark [Alabama] in the house of the poem 'The Wide Porch.' I remember John looking his records up at the hospital." Finlay's middle name, Martin, came from this uncle.

13. "If a Man Drive Out a Demon. . .": the source of this title in quotation marks has not yet been identified.

14. Southern poet and man of letters Allen Tate (1899–1979) was a profound influence on Finlay. Finlay met Tate on at least two

occasions. See Appendix D, "A Note on John Finlay and Allen Tate" by David Middleton on pages 190-193.

15. This event is recorded as having happened on March 13, 1938, the day after the Anschluss, Hitler's invasion of Austria.

16. Advent is the first season of the church year, a time of expectation and spiritual preparation in advance of Christ's birth at Christmas.

17. About "Off Highway 27" JoAnn Finlay Hall says, "This is a rural highway running from southeast Alabama to Florida. The towns would have been small when it was traveled, probably going to the beach." Highway 27 also runs between Enterprise and Ozark, Alabama—two important cities in Finlay's life.

18. The title of this poem is based on Jacob's wrestling with the angel in Genesis 32:26. The angel speaks, and Jacob answers: "And he said, Let me go, for the day breaketh. And he said, I will not let thee go, except thou bless me." JoAnn Finlay Hall says of this poem, "This would be Ma's mother, Granny Coston. She lived with Ma and was a very sweet, loving person. She told the stories John writes of being young during the War Between the States, something about Indians, and her job as a young girl to catch the chicken and cut [its] head off. It was her father in the poem 'Salt from the Winter Sea.'"

19. This stanza is from Finlay's "The Graves by the Sea," his translation of Paul Valéry's poem "Le Cimetière marin." Finlay's translation of Valéry is found on pages 116-120. "To David During Dark Times" was sent to David Middleton in the 1980s in an exchange of letters on difficulties facing the poet in the modern age. Finlay also wrote an essay on Valéry, "The *Otherness* of Paul Valéry," which can be found in *"With Constant Light": The Collected Essays and Reviews Along with Selections from the Diaries, Letters, and Other Prose of John Martin Finlay (1941–1991)*, pages 85-98.

Poems from Section V of *Mind and Blood* (1992)

20. Originally printed as Section V of *Mind and Blood* (1992). These are mature poems discovered among Finlay's papers but not included in *A Prayer to the Father* (1992). See Note 1 in the *A Prayer to the Father* prior section concerning the principle upon which the editors have sequenced posthumous gatherings of Finlay's poems.

21. Laguna Beach is in the Florida panhandle. For more on Finlay and Florida, see Note 20 on page 234. JoAnn Finlay Hall writes of this poem, "The bar I'm sure was called The Little Birmingham. I know John went there and this would have been in the 50's when the beach was not built up and the bar was very isolated."

22. Paul Valéry (1871–1945) was a French poet and essayist. Valéry spent most of his life in Paris. He was a friend of French Symbolist poet Stéphane Mallarmé. In 1925, he was elected to the Académie française. "Le Cimetière marin" is a poem on death, change, and contemplation. It is set in the cemetery of Valéry's hometown of Sète, where Valéry is buried. "Le Cimetèrie marin" appeared in Valéry's collection of verse *Charmes* (1922). Finlay made a diary entry about purchasing a copy of *Charmes* on December 14, 1973, upon first arriving in Paris: "I bought a copy of *Charmes*, the paper, Gallimard edition. On one page, the poetry: facing it an equal page of commentary. (I've reached at last my intellectual home!)." *"With Constant Light": The Collected Essays and Reviews Along with Selections from the Diaries, Letters, and Other Prose of John Martin Finlay (1941–1991)*, page 259. See also Note 19 just above for information on Finlay's essay on Valéry. Finlay commented on this translation in two letters to Donald E. Stanford. On January 30, 1982, Finlay wrote: "I am almost finished with the Valéry translation, which I have enjoyed a great deal. Didn't you once say that you considered Valéry the greatest poet in the 20th century? I can see why. At first I wanted to keep his rime scheme, but the blank verse of [Wallace Stevens' poem] *Sunday Morning* my first love, was too compelling." A letter to Stanford dated February 17, 1982, contains further remarks on Finlay's Valéry translation: "I'm sending in another envelope my translation of the Valéry. I gave up trying to translate the last line, which gave me untold difficulties. How would you translate it? And why the imperfect tense of 'picoraient'? By the way, I think Winters was wrong in thinking that the 'masse de calme, et visible réserve' refers to the sea. As I read the stanza, one has a series of apposites that finally modify 'édifice dans l'âme.' In other words, Valéry is talking not about the possibilities of the sea, but those of his intellect, the 'building' inside his own soul. Am I too far off base on this? And let me get your advice on another matter. The 9th stanza gave me a devil of a time, the one beginning 'Sais-tu fausse captive.' I finally and tentatively interpret it as being an address on the poet's part to both the sun itself and the sunlight reflected on the sea and the leaves of the trees surrounding the graveyard. Do you

think this is correct?" The John Finlay Papers, Louisiana State University. To David Middleton, Finlay wrote, on November 18, 1984: "I am enclosing the revised Valéry. . . . Would you tell me if the ending of the Valéry works for you? God knows I've worked long enough on it. Why do some pieces cost us so much and others don't? Surely there's some kind of obscure psychological blockage working in the deepest levels." In an earlier letter to David Middleton, November 9, 1981, Finlay made a comment inclusive of Valéry: "Valéry is beginning to irritate me. The whole aestheticism of the French is cloying after a while. And Valéry isn't interested in truth or goodness—*his* mind is kept pure of all *that* vague messy stuff. Well, so be it. The concentration [camps] were burning while he perfected his stylistic late masterpiece." Private collection of David Middleton.

23. Athena's simple shrine: See Note 70 on page 245. "The Autobiography of a Benedictine." French scholar Catharine Savage Brosman, commenting on the French original, writes of Valéry's "temple simple à Minerve" (which Finlay translates as "Athena's simple shrine"): "Despite quasi-Greek thoughts, a Greek figure, and Greek-based words, Valéry used the Roman name, perhaps for reasons of sound. 'Simple' was chosen probably for the half-rhyme with 'temple.' *Temple*, of course, is very close in spelling and sound to *temps* 'time'. They are probably cognate (see *Webster's Collegiate Dictionary*). This image is found in the line 'Stable trésor . . . .' The ocean is stable, despite its constant apparent movement (see line 2 of that stanza). Minerve/Athena is of course wisdom. The poem deals, among other things, with the intuitive self, versus the intellectual self (Zeno's reasoning, good but false since the arrow really does fly). The 'wisdom' would be that of stability, changelessness, constancy, vs. kinetic movement, human dynamism, the reality of human possibility in time (and thus death also)." Private note to David Middleton, May 12, 2018. Used with permission.

24. Zeno (ca. 490–ca. 430 B.C.) was a pre-Socratic Greek philosopher of the Eleatic School. He was best known for his paradoxes and as the inventor of the *reductio ad absurdum* (reduction to the absurd) method of argument. The Eleatic School was named after its home in the Greek city of Elea in southern Italy. Founded by Parmenides, the Eleatic School argued that the universal, unifying truth of all things, and of being itself, cannot be apprehended fully by the senses, which are limited, but such truth can be known by

way of conceptual thought. The Eleatics also denied the act of creation of the cosmos since logically being cannot proceed from non-being. The Eleatic One is Zeno.

25. Bacchic panther: Bacchus, the god of wine and fecundity, is sometimes depicted riding a panther or with a panther as companion. Chlamys: In ancient Greece, a chlamys was a short woolen cloak thrown over the shoulder and pinned with a brooch. The chlamys was worn by soldiers and hunters and by politicians on special public occasions.

26. Janet Lewis (1899–1998) was an American poet, novelist, and librettist. Born in Chicago, she was married to Yvor Winters (1900-68) and lived most of her adult life in California where she taught both at Stanford University and at Berkeley. Finlay admired Lewis' quietly understated yet powerful poems, most of which are in formal verse. Some of Lewis' poems are about American Indian life. Those poems almost certainly influenced Finlay's sequence of poems *The American Tragedies*, a typescript of which he sent to Lewis for comment. His letter to her is in Appendix E of this volume.

27. JoAnn Finlay Hall says of "Told from the Nineteenth Century," "This is about Annie Laurie Cullens who gave up marriage to care for her sister, Mary Emma. They lived in their family home in Ozark [Alabama] and it was said her father, Dr. Cullens, had contracted syphilis and that was why Mary Emma was 'crazy.' I was frightened of her as a child and remember her playing the piano beautifully." Annie Laurie Cullens was a local poet and lover of literature. She would give Finlay books and engaged him in literary, philosophical, and political discussions. For more on Finlay and Cullens see Jeffrey Goodman, "The Romance of Modern Classicism: Remarks on the Life and Work of John Finlay, 1941–1991," *The Alabama Literary Review*, 14:2, Fall 2000, 26. "Artemis (identified by the Romans with Diana), in Greek mythology [was] the daughter of Zeus and Leto, and sister of Apollo. . . . She was a goddess of wildlife, a virgin huntress, attended by a train of nymphs, and also a goddess of childbirth and of all very young things. She was also identified with the moon." Sir Paul Harvey, editor. *The Oxford Companion to Classical Literature*. Oxford: The Clarendon Press, 1937. 52.

28. Of "Through a Glass Darkly" JoAnn Finlay Hall has remarked, "This is about our great uncle, Waldo Emerson Ard. He was a big

part of our childhood memories as he lived in Ozark [Alabama]. Earlier in life he was an alcoholic and went on rampages, scaring mother and her sister. As he was recovering from a hangover, they read from the Bible to him. Grandmother made mother and her sister go to the tent revivals, which mother recalled as sometimes frightening." The title of Finlay's poem comes from St. Paul's First Letter to the Corinthians 13:12: "For now we see through a glass, darkly, but then face to face; now I know in part; but then shall I know even as also I am known." (KJV) In response to an invitation from Fred Hobson, editor of *The Southern Review*, to change the title of this poem because the same title was being used by the author of a work in the preceding issue, Finlay wrote on July 1, 1988: "I would change it but its source in St. Paul is appropriate to the 'Protestant' subject and so . . ."

29. JoAnn Finlay Hall says of this poem, "The woman is Mother [Jean Sorrell Finlay, 1920–2008]. It was very sad for the cows to be sold and John was living there then. It meant the barns were empty, the pastures with no cows and just an empty feeling. It was like the death of a working farm." For the story about John Finlay naming some of these cows after Greek goddesses, see the 1992 Preface above to *Mind and Blood*, page 25. In a letter of March 21, 1986, Finlay wrote to Lewis P. Simpson: "We still can't decide about selling the dairy. I really, after all, will miss the cows. They are like pets to us. I've even named some of my favorites after Greek gods and goddesses. The bulls are Zeus and Apollo, and a big white cow without one spot is Aphrodite. But farming as we know it is disappearing and we must face the reality." The John Finlay Papers, Louisiana State University. In a letter to David Middleton of September 25, 1989, Finlay wrote, "I realized that 'Slaughter' is really a retelling in an attenuated form of the episode of the killing of the cattle of Helios in *The Odyssey*." Private collection of David Middleton. Finlay's sisters, JoAnn Finlay Hall and Betty Finlay Phillips, recall that John "named a beautiful bull we had Prince Valiant" and that "he named other places on the farm Island of Desire, Queen's Castle, and Dead Man's Valley."

30. The title of this poem recalls those of Allen Tate's poems "Aeneas at Washington" and "Aeneas at New York." Andrew Littauer has commented on Finlay's poem: "This perfect epigrammatic achievement is a single heroic couplet in length. Finlay opposes the first line with its reference to Aeneas' oracle-prompted quest to found Rome with modern man's legacy of arbitrary and often

senseless violence. . . . This tiny poem concentrates its expansive theme by setting the noun and first end-rhyme 'home' with its sense of contented stasis against the verb and second end-rhyme 'roam' with its aura of active restlessness. Aeneas is an example of principle in action, and a man whose destiny is contrived by the gods with his active assistance. Modern man too often lacks the self-control and the guiding moral imperatives that would prevent him from committing heinous acts and atrocities." "The Mind and the Classical World in the Poetry of John Finlay." *In Light Apart: The Achievement of John Finlay*. Edited by David Middleton (Glenside, PA: The Aldine Press, 1999), 168.

31. Harry Duncan (1916–1997) was a widely admired American hand-press printer and publisher. Duncan's The Cummington Press published books by some of America's finest poets, including Wallace Stevens, Allen Tate, Yvor Winters, and Robert Lowell. In 1988, Duncan brought out Finlay's *The Salt of Exposure* on The Cummington Press.

Previously Uncollected Poems (2016)

32. From *John Finlay: A Commemoration Upon the Occasion of the Twenty-Fifth Anniversary of His Death: Selected and Edited from The John Finlay Papers and Other Sources* (2016). These are mainly earlier poems and drafts of later poems. On the gathering of these poems, see Note 1 above to the poems selected and sequenced in *A Prayer to the Father*.

33. Neely Bruce, a composer and longtime friend of John Finlay, is the sole source of the following poems: "Three Epigraphs," "Admonitions for a Pernoctation," "Dialogue," and "Instructions for Planting a Rose Bush." Bruce's recollected texts of these Finlay poems of the 1960s and his vocal compositions for the five poems may be viewed and heard online. Neely Bruce has stated in a note on the poems above that "These . . . poems were written while [Finlay] was a student in Tuscaloosa and are not found in his collected works. They were a gift to Jean Orr and Neely Bruce in the summer of 1964. The composer regrets that, even though he is a packrat, he cannot locate the originals. He has reconstructed the format of these pieces from what he can remember of their look on the page."

34. A pernoctation is a staying overnight in a certain place, especially

as a vigil.

35. This poem appeared in *Comment: The University of Alabama Review*, Winter 1965, 28. John Finlay was the editor of this volume.

36. This poem was published in *Comment,* Winter 1966, 2. The dedicatees have not yet been identified.

37. This poem was printed as the "First Prize" poem in *Comment*, Winter 1965 issue, 22. The poem's alternative title was "Vernal Equinox."

38. These words were added in Finlay's handwriting.

39. This poem was published in *Comment*, Spring 1967, 5.

40. Alternative wording in typescript: Creekwater is blackening

41. Alternative wording in typescript: Quiet as a cottonmouth

42. Alternative wording in typescript: In water blackening.

43. This poem appeared in *Comment,* Spring 1967, 5.

44. This poem is from a sequence entitled "Epigrams."

45. These poems are from a sequence entitled "Five Epigrams."

46. Alternative wording (handwritten): glance

47. See *Mind and Blood,* page 106, for two previously collected Advent epigrams.

48. Compare "This Fall, the South" to the longer version of this poem, "The Dead and the Season," in *Mind and Blood,* page 64.

49. Compare Finlay's poems, "Baudelaire in Belgium" and "Flaubert in Egypt," pages 98 and 100.

50. This poem first appeared posthumously in *The Epigrammatist,* 6.1, April 1995, 20.

51. Compare Finlay's poem "Off Highway 27," page 108.

52. For other versions of all or part of this poem see "Two Epigrams, II. A Fragment for the Fall" and "Stone and Fire,'" pages 63 and 99.

53. This poem was written in Baton Rouge in 1974 or 1975 for Finlay's friend Babs Green Zimmerman. Zimmerman has said that Finlay wrote this poem on the spot in response to her challenging remark that a poet ought to be able to compose spontaneously.

Additional Poems, Versions of Poems, Fragments, Lines, and Related Writings from the Diaries and Other Sources

54. The verse in this subsection is either collected or published here in book form for the first time. See Note 1 above to *A Prayer to the Father*.

55. This handwritten poem is signed and dated "John Finlay July 11, 1956." Finlay's sister JoAnn Finlay Hall writes of this poem composed by her brother at age fifteen that he inscribed it in a copy of William Wordsworth's poems published in The Athenaeum Press Series. Beside the poem, Finlay has partially paraphrased a statement from Wordsworth's "Preface to *Lyrical Ballads*" (1802): "Poetry is emotions remembered in tranquility."

56. Crumbling in the moon: Finlay considered these words as a possible line.

57. Another stanza? This is Finlay's note to himself on whether to add more lines to this earlier version of the poem.

58. This line and the four lines that follow are a partial draft of Finlay's poem "In Another Country," page 53.

59. This poem is a shorter version (or perhaps a partial draft) of Finlay's poem "In the Adriatic," page 33.

60. Finlay wrote this poem at age 21. The last line echoes Faulkner's Nobel Prize Speech delivered on December 10, 1950, in Stockholm, Sweden. See Lewis P. Simpson's comments on this poem in "John Finlay and the Situation of the Southern Writer," pages 199-213. The spelling of the word "drunkenly" as drunkenedly" in line 3 is that of Finlay.

61. Finlay left the last two handwritten lines unplaced in the poem. The editor of *Mind and Blood* made the decision in 1992 to insert these lines after line 12 in the typescript as that seemed the likeliest place for Finlay to have to put them.

62. Finlay made a note on this poem: "This is the first part of a long

poem that I have been working on, off and on, for the past years."

63. This is apparently the first version of "A Poem in Prose," printed above, page 145, which is in stanzas. Finlay often said that he wanted to write poetry that was "just above" the level of prose. These two versions of this poem—differing only in layout as a prose paragraph or three stanzas of unrhymed verse with varying line lengths—demonstrate Finlay's commitment to the plain style in poetry. See Note 14 in "Notes for the Perfect Poem" in Appendix A, page 182: "It must be plain."

64. Pelekas is a hillside village on the Greek island of Corfu.

65. This line and the nine lines that follow are a partial draft of the poem "In Another Country," page 53.

66. This line and the three lines that follow are a draft of lines for the poem "The Wide Porch," page 31.

67. This line and the nine lines that follow are a draft of lines for the poem "The Locked Wards," page 102.

68. This line and the twenty lines that follow are early draft-lines for Finlay's poem "Death in Asia Minor," pages 59-60. Athena and Orestes are major characters in Aeschylus' play *The Eumenides*. Athena casts the deciding vote in favor of the acquittal of Orestes at his trial in Athens on the charge of wrongfully killing his mother, Clytemnestra, for her murder of her husband (Orestes' father) Agamemnon, king of Mycenae (Argos) and leader of the Greek forces at Troy.

69. Perhaps Finlay means "unconventional."

70. The Erinyes (or Furies) were chthonic, winged female deities accompanied at times by snakes. They took revenge on those who violated the holy bonds of family. See Note 72 below on Orestes, Apollo, and Aeschylus' *Orestia* trilogy.

71. *Oedipus at Colonus* was the last play to be written—but the middle play in terms of chronology—of the three Theban plays by Sophocles (ca. 497/6 B.C.–406/5 B.C): *Oedipus Rex, Oedipus at Colonus*, and *Antigone*. Finlay has probably made this note about *Oedipus at Colonus* because of Oedipus' unintentional violation of holy ground in that play by entering a grove sacred to the Eumenides, another name for the Erinyes, or Furies.

72. *The Eumenides* is the final play in Aeschylus' three plays on Orestes—*The Orestia*. In *The Eumenides*, the Furies seek vengeance against Orestes for (as they see it) the unjust killing of his mother, with the blessing of Apollo. By Athena's deciding vote, Orestes is found not guilty, but the Furies, now named by Athena the Eumenides ("the kindly ones"), are henceforth to be revered by the Athenians. Also see Note 70 above.

73. The two lines that follow are drafts of lines for "Three Voices After the Greek, Sappho 2," 45.

74. Fränkel is most likely Eduard Fraenkel (1888–1970), the renowned German-British classical philologist, especially known for his work on the Roman comic playwright Plautus (ca. 254–184 B.C.) and on the *Agamemnon* by Greek tragedian Aeschlyus (525–456 B.C.).

75. This was a possible line for "Three Voices After the Greeks, Archilochus 1 and 2," page 45.

76. Compare this line and the thirteen lines that follow to Finlay's poem *"Origo mentis,"* pages 50-51.

77. This journal, purchased in Paris in 1973, contains entries from the 1970s and 1980s.

78. See Finlay's poem "Stone and Fire," page 99.

79. See Finlay's poem "Stone and Fire" and "Two Epigrams II. *A Fragment for the Fall*," pages 99 and 63.

80. For this line and the sixty-seven lines that follow see Finlay's poem "The Locked Wards," page 102.

81. "According to tradition, [St. Lucy] was a native of Syracuse who openly proclaimed her Christian faith by distributing her goods to the poor at the height of the Diocletian persecution. For this act she was denounced to the authorities by the young man to whom he had been betrothed by her parents, and suffered martyrdom in 303." F. L. Cross and E.A. Livingstone, editors. *The Oxford Dictionary of the Christian Church*. Oxford: Oxford University Press. 2nd edition, 1974. 842. This poem appeared in *Comment*, Winter 1968, 7.

82. This is a revised version of the poem, printed posthumously in

Louisiana English Journal, 3.2, New Series, 1996, 16. This version was not available for inclusion in *Mind and Blood* (1992).

83. This is an earlier version of the poem. It was published in *The Southern Review*, 9.4, Autumn 1973, 938. The revised version appears in *Mind and Blood*.

84. The draft versions just below of "Audubon at Oakley" and "To a Friend on His First Book" are from copies of *The Wide Porch and Other Poems* (1984) and *Between the Gulfs* (1986) which contain handwritten corrections and changes by Finlay. The originals of these copies are in The John Finlay Papers, LSU Libraries, Lower Mississippi Valley Special Collection, Baton Rouge, Louisiana. Finlay incorporated some, but not all, of these corrections into his typescript of *Mind and Blood*. These two poems are presented here as examples of the revision process, one poem from each chapbook.

85. See Note 15 above to *Mind and Blood* on the final version of this poem.

86. The word "and" is deleted in the version in *Mind and Blood*, page 44.

87. too many one-liners? Finlay added this query in the margin just after lines 15–17.

88. Finlay crossed out this line perhaps because of his concern expressed in Note 87.

89. Finlay wrote the word "terms" in the margin here as a possible substitute for "names."

90. Finlay considered an alternative final line: The salty vulgate of their Saxon names. In the first printing of the poem, in the autumn 1982 issue of *The Southern Review* (18:2, 357), the phrase "Saxon slang" was used in the final line of the poem. Possible line: In the crisp air, almost beyond all sound. Finlay contemplated adding this line near the end of the poem.

91. For information on this poem and friend, see Note 44 above in the *Mind and Blood* section.

92. Alternative line: this your book

93. Other possible final lines listed by Finlay:

And see consumed in them the private man.
And see a private man in them consumed.
And see its art consume a private friend.
Their art consumes the person of my friend.

94. "The Dead"—dated and signed "John Finlay, March 22, 1979," is an earlier version of "The Wide Porch" in *Mind and Blood*, page 31.

The American Tragedies:
A Chronology of Six Poems (1987)

1. Appendix E contains a letter from Finlay to Janet Lewis Winters to whom he sent a copy of *The American Tragedies: A Chronology of Six Poems*. Appendix F is David Middleton's note written for the chapbook printing of this sequence (R.L. Barth Press, 1997). Several of poems in this sequence appeared—sometimes in different versions—in other of Finlay's collections, but Finlay clearly intended for this sequence also to stand on its own as a separate work. This 1997 printing of *The American Tragedies* was based on the copy that Finlay sent to Janet Lewis Winters, who, after Finlay's death, provided her copy of this sequence to David Middleton. Notes on some of these poems appear above in the sections on *Mind and Blood, A Prayer to the Father* (1992), and *Uncollected Poems* (1992). Lewis P. Simpson is on record as having said that *The American Tragedies* seemed to promise an important new phrase and direction in Finlay's poetry and thought, but, due to Finlay's terminal illness, such a development was not to be.

Appendix A: Notes for the Perfect Poem by John Finlay

1. "Notes for the Perfect Poem" is from a journal Finlay kept in the 1960s–70s. Note 2 is probably repeated as Note 4 for emphasis.

Appendix B: The Mary Roberts Rinehart
Foundation Proposal by John Finlay

1. Finlay was not awarded a Rinehart grant nor did he write the long poem on Audubon's years in Louisiana, but he did write a short poem, "Audubon at Oakley," that appears in *Mind and Blood*, page 44. "Notes for the Perfect Poem" and this Rinehart proposal, taken together, are a major statement in prose of Finlay's

poetics. Mary Roberts Rinehart (1876–1958) was a writer of plays and of popular mystery stories and novels, including the novel *The Circular Staircase* (1908). She wrote for *The Saturday Evening Post* and served as the post's war correspondent in Belgium during World War I. She is credited with inventing the "Had-I-But-Known" and "The Butler Did It" approaches to mystery writing. The Mary Roberts Rinehart Awards were established by Rinehart's family after her death to assist aspiring writers.

2. These lines are taken from Finlay's poem "The Faun." See page 95.

3. "Circe [is] . . . a goddess living on the fabulous island of Aeaea. . . . She is very powerful in magic; her house is surrounded by wild beasts who fawn on new arrivals (. . . they are men changed by her spells) and [in *The Odyssey*] she turns Odysseus' men into swine." N.G.L. Hammond and H. H. Scullard, editors. *The Oxford Classical Dictionary.* Oxford: The Clarendon Press, 1969. 242.

Appendix D: A Note on John Finlay and Allen Tate by David Middleton (2018)

1. The inscription reads *Sancta Maria / Ora Pro Nobi*s (Holy Mary / Pray for us.)

Appendix E: A Letter from John Finlay to Janet Lewis Winters on *The American Tragedies* (1987)

1. This great-grandmother is recalled in the Finlay family as "Granny Coston."

2. This postscript is handwritten.

Appendix F: A Note on *The American Tragedies* by David Middleton (1987)

1. See Note 1 above to *The American Tragedies*.

Appendix G: Mind and Blood: John Finlay (1941–1991) by David Middleton

1. This essay was published as a tribute to Finlay in *The Southern Review*, 27.3, Summer 1991, 723–26. The following note was appended to the essay: "I wish to thank the following persons

who generously shared with me their memories of John Finlay: members of the Finlay family including Mrs. Jean Finlay (John's mother) and his sisters—Betty, JoAnn, and Patricia—and some of John's friends from LSU days including Terri Baker, William Bedford Clark, David Moreland, Betty Moss, and Wyatt Prunty as well as John's English friend, the poet Dick Davis."

Appendix H: John Finlay and the Situation of the Southern Writer by Lewis P. Simpson (1999)

1. This essay first appeared *In Light Apart: The Achievement of John Finlay*, 1999, 81–99.

2. The John Finlay Papers, Hill Memorial Library, Louisiana State University, Baton Rouge, Louisiana.

3. The Finlay Papers.

4. A copy of this inscription is in the Finlay Papers.

5. The Finlay Papers.

6. John Finlay, letter to the author, 12 May 1987, the *Southern Review* files, Louisiana State University, Baton Rouge, Louisiana.

7. See the letter of 5 August 1987 from Janet Lewis Winters to John Finlay, the Finlay Papers.

8. The Finlay Papers.

9. A copy of this inscription from the inside front cover of Finlay's copy of Allen Tate, *Collected Essays* (Denver: Swallow, 1959) is in the Finlay Papers.

10. David Middleton, letter to the author, 2 November 1996.

11. The Finlay Papers.

12. The Finlay Papers.

13. Allen Tate, *Essays of Four Decades* (Chicago: Swallow, 1968), 592.

14. Tate, *Essays of Four Decades,* 599–600.

15. Tate, *Essays of Four Decades,* 595–96, 600.

16. David Middleton, "'The Deathless Word': John Finlay and the Triumph over Gnosticism" in *Hermetic Light: Essays on the Gnostic Spirit in Modern Literature and Thought* by John Finlay (Santa Barbara, California: John Daniel and Company, 1994), 142.

17. Middleton, 142.

18. Tate, *Essays of Four Decades*, 16.

19. Tate, *Essays of Four Decades*, 16.

20. John Finlay, letters to the author, 19 July 1986 and 28 November 1986; the *Southern Review* files.

21. John Finlay, letter to the author, 21 August 1985; the *Southern Review* files.

22. Allen Tate, *Essays of Four Decades*, 574.

23. Allen Tate, *Essays of Four Decades*, 575–76.

24. The Finlay Papers.

25. Middleton, 146.

26. Walker Percy, *The Message in the Bottle* (New York: Farrar, Straus, Giroux, 1975), 114.

27. Allen Tate, "Mere Literature and the Lost Traveller," *Poetry* 135.2 (1979), 93–102; John Finlay, letter to the author, 21 August 1985.

28. John Finlay, letter to the author, 12 October 1986; the *Southern Review* files.

29. Middleton, 146.

30. John Finlay, letter to the author, 12 October 1986; the *Southern Review* files.

31. Middleton, 142.

Appendix I: The Poetry of John Finlay
by Donald E. Stanford (1991)

1. This memorial essay was published in *The Southern Review*, Summer, 1991, 27.3, 730–32.

Appendix J: "In Light Apart": The Achievement of John Finlay by David Middleton (1999)

1. Preface to The John Finlay issue of *Hellas 8.2*, 1997, 7–10. This issue was also published as a book: *In Light Apart: The Achievement of John Finlay*, Glenside, PA: The Aldine Press, 1999, edited by David Middleton.

Appendix K: Preface to *John Finlay: A Commemoration Upon the Occasion of the Twenty-Fifth Anniversary of His Death on February 17, 1991* by David Middleton (2016)

1. Privately printed in 2016 for members of the Finlay family and friends of John Finlay.

Appendix L: "The Break-In" by David Middleton

1. "The Break-In" appeared in *The Southern Review*. Autumn 2016. 52.4. 650–52.

John Finlay: A Bibliography (1962–2020)

Books, Chapbooks, Cards

The Wide Porch and Other Poems. 18 poems. Florence, Kentucky: Robert L. Barth, 1984.

Between the Gulfs. 17 poems. Notes by Finlay on the poems "*Origo mentis*" and "Death in Asia Minor." Florence, Kentucky: Robert L. Barth, 1986.

The Salt of Exposure. 19 poems. Omaha, Nebraska: Printed by Harry Duncan on The Cummington Press, 1988.

A Prayer to the Father: Poetry and Prose by John Finlay. Selected and edited from The John Finlay Papers by David Middleton. 25 poems. 9 excerpts from Finlay's diaries. Thibodaux, Louisiana: Blue Heron Press, 1992.

Mind and Blood: The Collected Poems of John Finlay. Edited and with a Preface by David Middleton. Santa Barbara, California: John Daniel and Company, 1992. This edition assembles the four earlier collections (with important late authorial emendations of several poems in the two Barth chapbooks) as well as 10 uncollected poems published in literary journals.

Hermetic Light: Essays on the Gnostic Spirit in Modern Literature and Thought. Introduction and six essays. Foreword by Lewis P. Simpson. Edited and with an Afterword by David Middleton. Santa Barbara, California: John Daniel and Company, 1994. Main title chosen by the editor from a line of one of Finlay's poems, "The Illumination of Arthur Rimbaud." Finlay's own title for this book, *Flaubert in Egypt and Other Essays*, could not be used for this edition.

Notes for the Perfect Poem. Four-page, one-fold card. 14 prose statements. Excerpt from Finlay's poem "*Origo mentis*" along with a brief historical comment on the background of the poem by David Middleton. Thibodaux, Louisiana: Blue Heron Press, 1994.

The Deathless Word: Christian Meditations from the Diaries and Poetry of John Finlay. Four-page, one-fold card. 4 journal entries. Excerpt from Finlay's poem "The Autobiography of a Benedictine." Thibodaux, Louisiana: Blue Heron Press, 1994.

The American Tragedies: A Chronology of Six Poems. Edited and with an Afterword by David Middleton. Edgewood, Kentucky: Robert L. Barth, 1997.

John Finlay: A Commemoration Upon the Occasion of the Twenty-Fifth Anniversary of His Death on February 17, 1991. Edited by David

Middleton and John P. Doucet. Privately printed in a limited edition for the Finlay family and friends of John Finlay, 2016. Previously unpublished and uncollected poems, letters, diary entries, and other prose from The John Finlay Papers at Louisiana State University and other sources.

Dissertation

"'The Unfleshed Eye': A Study of Intellectual Theism in the Poetry and Criticism of Yvor Winters." Directed by Donald E. Stanford. Louisiana State University, Baton Rouge, Louisiana, 1980. Now available online.

Previously Uncollected Essays

"Elizabeth Daryush." *The Dictionary of Literary Biography: British Poets, 1914–45*. Vol. 20. Edited by Donald E. Stanford. Detroit: Gale Research Company, 1983.109–12.

"The Night of Alcibiades." *The Hudson Review*. 47.1 (Spring 1994). 57–79.

"The Socratics and the Flight from This World." *Hellas*. 8.2 (Fall/Winter 1997). 63-80.

A Statement on Poetics. *Louisiana English Journal*. 32 (new series). 1996. 14–15. Three photographs of John Finlay. 12, 17, 18. The Mary Roberts Rinehart Foundation Proposal.

Previously Uncollected Poems

"The Return." *The Epigrammatist*. 6.1 (April, 1995). 20.

"Told from the Nineteenth Century." Revised version superseding the version available for publication in *Mind and Blood. Louisiana English Journal* 3.2 (new series). 1996. 16.

Book Reviews

"N. Scott Momaday's *Angle of Geese*." Review of *Angle of Geese* by N. Scott Momaday. *The Southern Review* 11.3 (Summer 1975). 658–61.

"Elizabeth Daryush." Review of *Collected Poems* by Elizabeth Daryush. *The Southern Review* 14.2 (Spring 1978). 404–08.

"Robert Bridges." Review of *In the Classic Mode: The Achievement of Robert Bridges* by Donald E. Stanford. *PN Review* (Manchester, England) 6.6 (1979). 78-79.

"Dick Davis' *Seeing the World.*" Review of *Seeing the World* by Dick Davis. *The Southern Review* 17.3 (Summer 1981). 654–56.

"Grosvenor Powell's *Language as Being.*" Review of *Language as Being in the Poetry of Yvor Winters* by Grosvenor Powell. *The Southern Review* 17.4 (Autumn 1981). 1001–03.

"The Poetry of Raymond Oliver." Review of *Entries* and *To Be Plain* by Raymond Oliver, *The Southern Review* 19.1 (Winter 1983). 178–80.

"Three from the Symposium." Review of *Witnesses* by Edgar Bowers, *The Birthday of the Infanta* by Janet Lewis, and *Many Houses* by Charles Gullans. *The Southern Review* 19.1 (Winter 1983). 181–83.

Other

Strode, Hudson. *Jefferson Davis: Private Letters, 1823-1889.* New York: Harcourt, Brace and World, 1966. "I am indebted to John M. Finlay, Instructor in English at Alabama College, for valuable assistance in the selecting and discarding of letters." Comment by Strode on page 566 (Acknowledgments). Alabama College is now the University of Montevallo.

The Cartesian Lawnmower and Other Poems by Don Stanford. Florence, Kentucky: Robert L. Barth, 1984. Chosen, edited, and arranged by John Finlay. [unattributed].

"Of Harry Duncan" in *A Garland for Harry Duncan* (Austin, Texas: W. Thomas Taylor, 1989). 25.

Untitled jacket comment for the paperback edition of *The Burning Fields* [poetry] by David Middleton. Baton Rouge, Louisiana: LSU Press, 1991. Finlay's last writing, dictated from his sickbed in August of 1990.

"After Samuel Johnson's Latin Poem to Thomas Lawrence, M.D." and "After Johnson's *Summe Pater.*" Translations from the Latin. *Samuel Johnson: Selected Latin Poems Translated by Various Hands.* Edited by Bob Barth. Edgewood, Kentucky: Robert L. Barth, 1987; 1995. 11, 13.

Manuscripts, Papers, Library, Future Projects

The John Finlay Papers. LSU Libraries, Lower Mississippi Valley Special Collections, Louisiana State University, Baton Rouge, Louisiana. These papers contain Finlay's published books, his journals, copies of *Comment* (the University of Alabama [Tuscaloosa] literary journal Finlay edited and contributed to in the years 1962-67, including an interview with Eudora Welty), miscellaneous items, letters to Finlay from poets such as Robert L. Barth, Edgar Bowers, and Janet Lewis, and letters from Finlay to Janet Lewis, David Middleton, Helen Pinkerton, Donald E. Stanford, and others. Letters from Finlay to Lewis P. Simpson are in *The Southern Review* files and the Simpson Papers at LSU. Books from John Finlay's library containing significant marginalia are in the possession of David Middleton (Finlay's literary executor).

Works About John Finlay

Barbarese, J. T. "Modernity and the Divided Intellect." Review-essay on *Hermetic Light: Essays on the Gnostic Spirit in Modern Literature and Thought* by John Finlay. *The Sewanee Review* 102.3 (Summer 1994). 486–92.

Barth, R. L. "'Plainest Naked Truth': John Finlay's *The Salt of Exposure.*" Review of *The Salt of Exposure* by John Finlay. *The Southern Review* 25.1 (Winter 1989). 255–58.

Barth, R. L. Review of *Mind and Blood: The Collected Poems of John Finlay. The Classical Outlook* 70.4 (Summer 1993). 148–49.

Clark, William Bedford. "Testament of a Traditionalist." Review of *Mind and Blood: The Collected Poems of John Finlay. The Sewanee Review* 101.2 (Spring 1993). lxix-lxx.

Clark, William Bedford. "'The Sweated Line': The Unclaimed Legacy of John Finlay." A review-essay on *Mind and Blood: The Collected Poems of John Finlay. Explorations: The Levy Humanities Series, University of Southwestern Louisiana* VII (1993). 53–61.

Davenport, Guy. Review of *Mind and Blood: The Collected Poems of John Finlay. Louisiana Literature* 101 (Spring 1993). 70–72.

Goodman Jeffrey. "Heroic and Tragic Story: Spotlight Shines on Poet's Work Several Years after His Death." *The Mobile Register.* 25 January 1998. 5D.

Goodman, Jeffrey. "The Romance of Modern Classicism: Remarks on the Life and Work of John Finlay, 1941–1991." *The Alabama Literary Review* 14:2 (Fall 2000). 25–49. This essay is also available on online.

Hammond, Ralph. [Poet Laureate of Alabama]. "John Finlay's Flowering of Poetry." Review of *Mind and Blood: The Collected Poems of John Finlay. Alabama Arts* 11.1 (Spring 1993). 36.

Jacket comments by Donald E. Stanford, Janet Lewis, Dick Davis, and R. L. Barth for *Mind and Blood: The Collected Poems of John Finlay.* Santa Barbara, California: John Daniel and Company, 1992. Back of dust jacket.

Middleton, David. "With Constant Light: The Poetry of John Finlay."

Review of *The Wide Porch and Other Poems* by John Finlay. *The Southern Review* 21.2 (Spring 1985). 558–63.

Middleton, David. "Featured Poet: John Finlay." *Poetry Pilot*. The Academy of American Poets. (January 1990). 3–9.

Middleton, David, editor. *A Garland for John Finlay*. Thibodaux, Louisiana: Blue Heron Press, 1990. Poems by 20 American and British poets; comments on Finlay's poetry by Janet Lewis and Donald E. Stanford; an essay on Finlay's prose by Lewis P. Simpson; and "John Finlay: A Bibliography (1971–1991)."

Middleton, David. Review of *The Salt of Exposure* by John Finlay. *The Classical Outlook* 68.3 (Spring 1991). 106,108.

Middleton, David. "Blood and Mind: John Finlay (1941–1991)." *The Southern Review* 27.3 (Summer 1991). 723–26.

Middleton, David. "Preface" to *Mind and Blood: The Collected Poems of John Finlay*. Santa Barbara, California: John Daniel and Company, 1992.15–18.

Middleton, David. "'The Deathless Word': John Finlay and the Triumph over Gnosticism." Afterword to *Hermetic Light: Essays on the Gnostic Spirit in Modern Literature and Thought*. Santa Barbara, California: John Daniel and Company, 1994. 141–57.

Middleton, David, editor. *In Light Apart: The Achievement of John Finlay*. Glenside, PA: The Aldine Press, 1999. Essays and poems by Finlay and by various hands and with a descriptive bibliography of works by and about Finlay, including the preface "In Light Apart: The Achievement of John Finlay," pages 7–10, by David Middleton.

Middleton, David. "John Finlay." Entry on Finlay in the *Encyclopedia of Alabama*, 2009. Online.

Middleton, David. "John: An Anglican Meditation on Literary Gifts and Giving." *The Anglican*. 41.3 Pentecost 2013. 36–40. The story of *A Garland for John Finlay*.

Middleton, David. "In Allen Hall: LSU, *The Southern Review*, and Baton Rouge." *The Southern Review* 52.4, 2016. 645–49. Includes reminiscences of Finlay at LSU in the 1970s–80s.

Middleton, David. "The Break-In." *The Southern Review* 52.4, 2016. 650–52. Poem on Finlay and a story about him from his years at LSU as a graduate student in the 1970s.

Oliver, Judy. "Alabama Poet Expresses Creative Vision, Originality." Review of *Mind and Blood: The Collected Poems of John Finlay*. *The Montgomery Advertiser* 13 December 1992. 6F.

Simpson, Lewis P. "John Finlay and the Situation of the Southern Writer." *In Light Apart: The Achievement of John Finlay*. Edited by David Middleton. Glenside, PA: The Aldine Press, 1999. 81-99.

Simpson, Lewis P. "The Dark Rooms of John Finlay." *The Southern Review* 27.3 (Summer 1991). 727–29. Also printed in *A Garland for John Finlay* and as "Foreword" to *Hermetic Light: Essays on the Gnostic Spirit in Modern Literature and Thought* by John Finlay.

Stanford, Donald E. "Dense Poems and Socratic Light." Review of *Mind and Blood: The Collected Poems of John Finlay*. *The Southern Review* 29.1 (Winter 1993). 186–91.

Stanford, Donald E. "The Poetry of John Finlay." *The Southern Review* 27.3 (Summer 1991). 730–32.

Stanford, Donald E. "The Poetry of David Middleton and John Finlay." *Hellas: A Journal of Poetry and the Humanities* 7.1 (1996). 10–11.

Stefanescu, Alina. "Lyrics and Life of Alabama Poet, John Finlay." September 19, 2012. Online.

Wildman, John Hazard. Review of *The Wide Porch and Other Poems* by John Finlay. *South Central Review* 1.4 (Winter 1984). 106–07.

Wilmer, Clive. Obituary for John Finlay. *PN Review* (Manchester, England) 17 (July/August 1991). 3–4.

Wilmer, Clive. "Darkness Visible." Review of *Mind and Blood: The Collected Poems of John Finlay*. *PN Review* 95 (January/February 1994). 60–61.

A Note on The John Finlay Papers at Louisiana State University

The John Finlay Papers (Mss. 4415) are located in the Louisiana and Lower Mississippi Valley Collections, Hill Memorial Library, LSU Libraries, Baton Rouge, Louisiana 70803. Telephone: 1-225-578-6544. Anyone possessing poems, letters, or other writings by, about, or related to John Finlay, as well as photographs or recordings or other materials, is invited to consider placing them in The John Finlay Papers. A detailed catalogue of items already in The John Finlay Papers may be obtained from Archives at Louisiana State University.

These papers contain the diaries, essays, poems, published books and chapbooks (including copies with late authorial corrections), notes and drafts, book reviews both by and about Finlay, secondary criticism, miscellaneous items, Finlay family letters, and correspondence between John Finlay and a number of literary figures including Robert L. Barth, Edgar Bowers, Dick Davis, Andrew Lytle, David Middleton, Lindon Stall, Donald E. Stanford, Lewis P. Simpson, Clive Wilmer, Janet Lewis Winters, and others.

We are ready to assist any scholar who is interested in the life and works of John Finlay.

David Middleton
Literary Executor for John Finlay
Poet in Residence Emeritus
Nicholls State University
Thibodaux, Louisiana

davidmiddleton@charter.net
david.middleton@nicholls.edu

John P. Doucet, Ph.D.
Dean, College of Sciences and Technology
Nicholls State University
Thibodaux, Louisiana

john.doucet@nicholls.edu

An Entry from John Finlay's Paris Diary (1973)

Dec. 24, 1973. Christmas Eve. . . . On the Metro or rather in the stations underground, I got my first glimpse of Metro life. There were "hippies" singing and begging for money. One old woman who, I think, was drunk beyond consciousness, was pathetically trying to sleep on crumpled-up bags and old clothes which were piled up on the Metro bench. No position suited her. One hand was extended and it moved awfully here and there, making meaningless gestures. Her cold poverty and discomfort were overwhelming. Once she turned over and in the full glare of the electric light, with her eyes closed and her lips moving silently, she made or rather tried to make the sign of the cross. Later, after the party, a small group of us went to Midnight Mass at St. Germain l'Auxerrois, which featured Gregorian music. It was the bells of this church which gave the signal for the massacre of St. Bartholomew. And on the second Sunday of every month, a mass is celebrated for the souls of departed poets.

—John Martin Finlay (1941–1991)

DAVID MIDDLETON

Until his retirement in June of 2010, David Middleton served for thirty-three years as Professor of English, Poet-in-Residence, Distinguished Service Professor, Alcee Fortier Distinguished Professor, and Head of the Department of Languages and Literature at Nicholls State University in Thibodaux, Louisiana. He was made Professor Emeritus at Nicholls in January of 2011. In August of 2014, Middleton was named the first Poet in Residence Emeritus at Nicholls.

Middleton has served as John Finlay's literary executor since Finlay's death in 1991. Works by Finlay that Middleton has edited and seen into print, as well as Middleton's own publications on Finlay, are listed in the bibliography of this volume.

Middleton's books of verse include *The Burning Fields* (LSU Press, 1991), *As Far as Light Remains* (The Cummington Press [Harry Duncan], 1993), *Beyond the Chandeleurs* (LSU Press, 1999), *The Habitual Peacefulness of Gruchy: Poems After Pictures by Jean-François Millet* (LSU Press, 2005), and *The Fiddler of Driskill Hill: Poems* (LSU Press, 2013). Middleton has also published several chapbooks of verse including *The Language of the Heart*, (Louisiana Literature Press, 2003), which won an award from *The Advocate* (Baton Rouge) as the best book of verse by a Louisianian for 2003. In March of 2014, *The Fiddler of Driskill Hill* won Second Honorable Mention from the Louisiana Library Association as Best Book of the Year for 2013 by a Louisianian or about Louisiana. Middleton's latest collection of verse, *Outside the Gates of Eden*, will appear in 2020 on Measure Press.

In April of 2006 Middleton won The Allen Tate Award for best verse published in *The Sewanee Review* in 2005. In November of 2006 Middleton won the State of Louisiana Governor's Award for Outstanding Professional Artist for 2006.

Middleton's verse has appeared in *The Alabama Literary Review, The Anglican, The Anglican Theological Review, The Classical Outlook, Chronicles: A Magazine of American Culture, Critical Quarterly, Europe, The Formalist, Louisiana Literature, The Louisiana Review, The Lyric, Measure: A Review of Formal Poetry, Modern Age, The North American Anglican, POEM, The Sewanee Review, The Sewanee Theological Review, The South Carolina Review, The Southern Review, Xavier Review*, and elsewhere.

Middleton has served as poetry editor for *The Classical Outlook, The Anglican Theological Review, The Louisiana English Journal,* and *Modern Age* as well as an advisory editor at *Measure: A Review of Formal Poetry.*

JOHN P. DOUCET

Then in his twenties, John Doucet became the youngest poetry contributor to *A Garland for John Finlay* (Blue Heron Press, 1990). Prior to that time, Doucet studied poetry under David Middleton as a undergraduate student at Nicholls State University. Doucet is now Dean of the Colleges of Sciences and Technology, Director of Coastal Initiatives, Alcee Fortier Distinguished Professor, and McIlhenny Professor of Human and Environmental Genetics.

Doucet's poetry has appeared in *Drastic Measures*, *The Epigrammatist*, and *Louisiana English Journal*, as well as other journals. He is author of the chapbooks *A Local Habitation and a Name: Poems from the Lafourche Country* (Blue Heron Press, 1995) and the forthcoming *A Grumble of Pugs*. Since 2016, he has developed a series of lecture-readings from his portfolio of formalist poetry on scientific topics. The lectures, entitled "Motion of the Outer Rime" (after the line Yvor Winters' "The Invaders"), "A Night or Two in Neander," "Lincoln's Thalamus and other Gray Matters," and "Variants of Unknown Significants" have been features of successive annual meetings of the Louisiana Academy of Sciences. A selection of these poems will appear later in 2020 in *Chronicles: A Magazine of American Culture*.

In the decade between 1993 and 2003, Doucet wrote and produced 13 plays immersed in Louisiana Cajun history and culture and enjoyed a four-year residency at the Oak Alley Outdoor Dinner Theater in Vacherie, Louisiana. In 1993, his play, "*Tant que Durera la Terre*," which chronicled survival of his great-great grandfather's family during the Great Cheniere Hurricane of 1893, was awarded the Louisiana Native Voices and Visions Playwriting Award. He is past recipient of the Louisiana Division of the Arts Fellowship in Playwriting.

Doucet is also contributing editor of the history anthologies, *Lafourche Country II: The Heritage and Its Keepers* and *Lafourche Country III: Annals and Onwardness*, as well as senior editor of the *Proceedings of the Louisiana Academy of Sciences* and columnist for *Point of Vue* magazine (Houma, Louisiana).

www.ingramcontent.com/pod-product-compliance
Lightning Source LLC
Chambersburg PA
CBHW070757020526
44118CB00036B/1843